Faith, Money & Tea

Faith, Money & Tea

The Ultimate Guide to Financial Rest!

Michelle Elliott

Freedom World Press, Inc
P.O. Box 6424
Douglasville, Georgia 30154

I dedicate this book to the cherished memories of my late grandmothers, Celian Hyder, and Ethel Marie Moore, and my beloved Aunt, Mary Dance. They had a significant influence on the person I am today. I learned so much from their unwavering faith and convictions, regardless of external opinions. They taught me to be strong in my faith and fully anchored in my beliefs. It has left an indelible mark on my journey. Their influence on my life surpasses what they could have ever imagined.

Contents

Acknowledgments

FIRST AND FOREMOST, I WOULD FIRST LIKE TO GIVE thanks to god. I cannot express enough my gratefulness for what He has done in my life. When I was deep in debt, God didn't leave me there. He pulled me out of the miry clay and set my feet upon a rock! God made a way out of no way. When I thought I might never get out of debt, God opened the Red Sea and set me free. I can't thank Him enough.

I am so grateful for my family. They inspire me more than they will ever know. I could not have finished this book without them! I want to acknowledge my husband, James. Writing a book requires much sacrifice, and he has genuinely been supportive. He always assures me that I can accomplish anything and supports whatever I do in any way he can.

I also greatly thank my children, Jasmine, Jordan, and Justin, who continuously asked how I was doing and checked my progress. They were my pillars of strength, always there to propel me forward; they helped to push me toward the book's completion.

I crafted this book while getting my master's degree in Christian Ministry at Oral Roberts University. I am deeply grateful to my professors and classmates who tremendously supported this book. They were a source of strength and encouragement as they motivated me toward a strong finish.

Finally, I want to thank all my family, friends, and those who attended my seminars, workshops, and conferences. You have all encouraged me to write and share this book with the world.

Introduction

I N 2010, I WAS BURIED IN CREDIT CARD DEBT THAT had grown to $100,000 and facing financial disaster! I realized that I had more debt than money in the bank and not enough money to pay my bills, which meant I was bankrupt. Why did I accumulate such a massive amount of debt? Unfortunately, I was well-trained by the world to use "other people's money" or OPM. I learned how to use borrowed capital to start businesses, buy real estate, and flip houses. I learned to leverage money borrowed from credit cards and lines of credit to create investment opportunities rather than using cash.

It took an economic recession to help me realize that I had no business being in debt. I discovered that using other people's money has severe risks and consequences. Everything was good if I was making gains and paying my creditors, but when I experienced losses, I found myself trapped in debt and struggling to make my monthly obligations. My back was against the wall. No one could help me with such overwhelming debt but God. So, I prayed and began to seek God's wisdom for answers.

I took a three-year spiritual journey to search the Scriptures to discover what the Word of God said about money and debt. As I studied the Bible, I found many passages warning about the consequences of borrowing money. I became thoroughly convinced that being in debt is not God's will for me or any other Christian.

Unfortunately, debt has become accepted as a usual way of life in America. Many Christians cannot imagine their life without debt. They are accustomed to borrowing money through loans and credit and making monthly payments. To think of acquiring things without a loan would make most people cringe. They couldn't imagine being able to afford a house, a car, an education, or anything without small, manageable, easy payments.

This book will take you on my journey from being in $100,000 of credit card debt to becoming debt-free and living by faith. By sharing my financial journey, I hope you can see your story within my story and get on the right path toward financial freedom.

Can you imagine your life with NO DEBT? NO mortgage, NO car payment, NO credit card debt, and NO student loans? You may be thinking, "Everybody uses debt." And it's true. The reliance on debt has become an inherent part of modern life for most individuals and households. In its various forms, debt has enabled people to achieve their goals, sustain a living, and fund their desires. Some people borrow during challenging times to pay for emergencies or unexpected expenses, such as medical bills or job loss. Others use debt as a tool and a resource to fund their everyday living.

But what does God say? Well, God says, *"Thou shall not borrow!"* The Bible tells us not to be conformed to this world's ways. We must renew our minds with the Word and transform our lives to align with what God says and what pleases Him. The Bible also gives tragic examples of what happens in the lives of people in bondage to debt payments.

If you read this book with your spiritual eyes open, you will see that living in debt is a serious spiritual issue and that freedom from debt is the will of God. You will also discover what the Bible says about money and debt. You may be surprised to learn how many Scriptures warn us against borrowing money. You will find that debt contradicts God's plan for meeting our needs. There are two competing financial systems operating in this universe: the world's economy and God's. One leads to bondage and frustration; the other leads to rest and peace.

In 2010, I stopped using credit and loans completely. I learned to trust God for everything! I learned to follow biblical principles of money management instead of man's advice. I went from being maxed out in credit card debt, worried and anxious about how I would pay my bills, to a life of financial freedom.

Attaining financial freedom is not merely about accumulating vast amounts of wealth. Instead, it is about having sufficient resources to live comfortably, meet your needs, and bless others. Generosity and compassion are inherent human traits that bring profound joy and fulfillment. Most people desire to help those in need but can't or don't feel they can because of their own financial constraints and burdens.

Financial freedom is a state of being that most people strive for throughout their lives. Many people seek out good-paying jobs, pursue higher education, or open a business to accumulate wealth so they don't have to worry about money. They go about it incorrectly by using debt to fund these pursuits. However, the goal should be to attain these aspirations gradually and steadily by adhering to a structured plan that keeps you out of debt and financially free.

One of the most significant benefits of financial freedom is the ability to pursue your purpose, passions, and hobbies without worrying about the associated costs. Whether it's getting an education, traveling, engaging in creative pursuits, or simply enjoying the little pleasures of life, financial freedom opens the door to experiences that might have been otherwise unattainable. For instance, I never sat down daily to drink hot tea when I was in a heap of debt. I didn't have time! I was too busy running after the next opportunity so that I could keep my bills paid. I couldn't rest!

Savoring a hot cup of tea embodies the idea of sitting back and relaxing while appreciating the small joys in life without being preoccupied with financial worries. Achieving financial freedom gives you the luxury to sit back and enjoy simple pleasures. While sitting down to enjoy a hot cup of tea may seem like a trivial pursuit, it symbolizes the essence of a stress-free, contented life that can be achieved by getting your financial house in order through financial planning, discipline, and making wise financial decisions based on biblical truth. Sitting back with a hot cup of tea represents peace, rest, and freedom!

What are some things you want to do but can't because you have debts to pay? Financial freedom empowers you to choose activities that align with your values and aspirations. It enables you to prioritize personal growth, spend quality time with loved ones, and contribute to meaningful causes. Such empowerment is liberating because it allows you to create a life that reflects your true desires rather than being constrained by financial obligations.

In 2012, God led me to start a class to help others get out of debt and live in financial freedom. I have held many financial freedom seminars and conferences where I have coached and encouraged thousands of people to go debt-free. I felt a sense of urgency from God to show others what He was showing me about debt. I could hear Him say, *"Remove the stumbling block out of the way of my people"* (Isaiah 57:14). That stumbling block is debt—brought on by anxiety for things, materialism, and covetousness.

Debt is a trap, an insurmountable obstacle that keeps God's people living paycheck to paycheck, constantly chasing after financial security and prosperity instead of living by true faith in God as their help and source. I was led to teach biblical financial literacy, focusing on stewardship, contentment, giving, and wise financial management.

At the core of what I teach lies the concept of stewardship. Understanding that God is the ultimate owner of all things empowers us to become responsible managers of the resources He has entrusted to us. Psalm 24:1 says, *"The earth is the Lord's, and everything in it, the world, and all who live in it."* This mindset shifts our perspective from an attitude of possession to one of gratitude and responsibility. Recognizing that we are mere stewards challenges us to use our finances wisely, making decisions that align with God's purposes and the well-being of others. It encourages us to manage our income, expenditures, and investments with integrity, accountability, and long-term vision.

While I was writing this book, a health pandemic caused a global financial crisis and economic slowdown. In America today, we are experiencing inflation, unrest in financial markets, supply chain shortages, high gas prices, and higher prices for food, energy, and housing. Everything is getting more expensive, putting an enormous financial strain on the government, families, and individuals. More than ever, people need to know who to turn to in times like these. Christians and everybody else must understand that no man, president, or government can promise to give you a secure life, peace, happiness, and financial stability like God.

In this book, you will discover the spiritual and practical principles of financial freedom and stewardship that I used to get out of debt. I discuss the role of spiritual habits necessary to get out of debt and stay out. These practices will break the spiritual chains of bondage caused by financial mismanagement. I learned to depend only on God, manage my money well, and prepare for such times. I have not been impacted financially by this current recession because I have no debt.

You will also find within these pages the practical principles that helped me change my financial behaviors to be empowered to prosper. Learning to walk by faith and not by sight has made all the difference in my life. I took my focus off money and placed all my hope and trust in God. I am fully convinced that God will supply all my needs—and yours, too, if you trust Him.

I wrote this book for Christian believers. However, this information is useful for anyone who is tired of financial struggle and uncertainty. The principles in this book are essential for people who are in debt or living paycheck to paycheck—even those with a great career and a good income. It doesn't matter how secure you feel; financial hardship can occur suddenly and without warning, as it did for me. If you are in debt, it only takes the loss of a job, a reduction in income, a medical emergency, the loss of a spouse, a pandemic, or an economic recession to end up in financial panic or poverty.

As you read, you will learn that getting out of debt and having a plan for managing your money will bring you ultimate financial peace and rest! You will also see words like oppression, bondage, evil, and sin. Don't allow these words to offend you or make you feel condemned. Too often, the Word of God is sugarcoated to make everybody comfortable. But not being honest about our problems, especially our financial problems, will not bring about change.

I am debt-free today because I was open to the absolute truth! It is time to pull the wool off the lies taught about money and building wealth. If you want to be free from debt and financial bondage, only the truth will set you free! This book is not for you if you want something other than the biblical truth about money and debt. But if you desire to discover true financial peace and rest, sit back with a cup of tea and read on!

Chapter 1

My Financial Crisis

A T THE BEGINNING OF 2010, I LIVED WHAT MANY would call the American Dream. I enjoyed being a stay-at-home mom and taking care of my three children. We lived in a beautiful six-bedroom, four-bath home with a picket fence and a dog. We drove nice cars and had money saved in the bank. My husband had a great job in corporate America as an information technology manager. He also owned a small business, and we had investment income. I worked with clients from time to time as a real estate agent. I got my license mainly because my husband and I invested in real estate.

In 2004, my husband started purchasing rental properties. By 2008, we had six fully rented properties. These properties were a great source of additional income. We were making money, able to invest, and had money saved in the bank. We took great vacations every year, which allowed us to relax from work and spend time together as a family.

We were living the good life!

Life was good until the 2008 stock market crash and economic recession! This financial crisis lasted several years and affected people in the United States and worldwide. Many causes triggered the recession, including excessive risk-taking by U.S. banks and the subprime mortgage crisis. Several banking and financial institutions experienced massive losses, which caused them to collapse. There was reason for alarm about the failure of vital financial institutions because they provide the loans and credit that drive the U.S. economy. When banks could no longer lend, it exacerbated the economic slowdown, which led to a government bailout of these institutions. The government also released a stimulus package to help the economy rebound.

It was like a perfect storm. The mortgage crisis resulted from too much borrowing; predatory lenders gave loans to high-risk borrowers by offering mortgage loan incentives and easy terms. Lenders encouraged these borrowers to take on risky home loans with the expectation of refinancing later at a lower rate. However, house prices and values started to drop, and the interest rates began to rise, making it difficult or impossible to refinance these bad loans. Borrowers began to walk away from their homes and defaulted on their mortgages, which led to many foreclosures. For many households, the situation was grim. People were being laid off from their jobs, and incomes were falling.

Now, back to my story.

The economy began to have a significant effect on the renters who were living in our rental properties. They were losing their jobs and falling behind on paying their bills. Our tenants were late on their rent, one by one. Within six months, it reached the point that none of our renters had paid their rent on time. They had to move out, one after the other. These were relatively new properties when most of these tenants moved in. The homes had freshly painted walls, new carpet, and some had new appliances. But as the renters moved out, many left trash, ruined carpet, holes in the walls, broken appliances, and unpaid rent. Unfortunately, these properties were mortgaged. So, not only were we spending money to renovate, repair, and replace items in these homes, we were paying four mortgages simultaneously! (Two properties had no mortgage.) We had to make these mortgage payments for about six months as we tried to find new renters.

During the recession, many people abandoned their homes and defaulted on mortgages, but we persevered. We made every payment on time directly from our savings account. These were not small mortgages. I am talking about mortgage payments over $700 per month each that we paid out of our bank account—not using borrowed money, but cash. Plus, we had spent much time and money repairing and preparing these properties to be rented again.

As I watched our account balance get lower, I quickly realized that something was wrong with what we were doing. Something inside told me that this situation was about more than tenants moving out and leaving us holding the bag. Deep inside, I felt something more was happening than a bad economy. I knew there had to be a more significant issue at hand. I was missing some essential godly wisdom about money because our situation went from bad to worse.

While we were dealing with the rental properties, I was facing another financial battle. I depended on part of our investment income to pay my credit card bills. I had credit card bills, and my husband had credit card bills. However, we never discussed how much each of us owed. We had the money to make the payments, so we paid them. Before the recession, when my bills came in, I paid them every month with no problem. But the income that I depended on had utterly dried up. My credit card bills kept coming in the mail every week, but the money to pay them was no longer coming in. At one point, it seemed the statements came in faster than before. I had 11 open credit card accounts and credit lines at one time! I didn't even realize I had so many. Every time I looked up, there was a new statement in the mail. Fear and anxiety began to set in.

Before the recession, I paid little attention to the total amount I owed on my credit cards. When the statements came in, I looked at the minimum amount due and just paid it. I did this for all the cards except American Express; I paid that bill in full every month because that is what the card required. For the others, I did not look at the total amount due even though I knew the balance was rising in the back of my mind because the minimum payments were rising. I had this warped faith that something big was going to happen. I had this flawed faith that God would bless me with some excellent business opportunity or a way to bring some remarkable income, and the debt would not matter. I thought that one day I would pay it all off. But now reality was setting in. I was in a lot of debt!

Forced to Face My Debt

As I said, I never really took the time to look at my credit card statements. I just mailed a check to pay the minimum balance. But I was now faced with a dilemma. I didn't have a regular 9-to-5 job where I received a steady income. My income came from our investments. We were investors, and that revenue had dried up! But now I was faced with sitting down and looking at it all. And that was not easy.

I was worried.

The money coming in every month that covered my bills had ended. The investment money and the world economy were in a "recession." We still had money in the bank, but it was our savings, which wasn't enough to cover the mortgages and my debts.

I could no longer ignore my debt. As the bills came in, I reluctantly began adding up the total amounts I owed. I had one card with a balance of $3,000. The next bill that came in was $4,777. I had another statement that showed $13,512 owed. Then there was one that was a whopping $20,345. Another bill came, then another. On top of all that credit card debt, I had taken out a student loan when I returned to college to take some additional undergraduate courses. It totaled a little over $5000.00. I didn't realize that my debt had climbed to over $100,000.

It was hard to believe that I owed that much money, most of which was credit card debt and credit lines. I had no car notes and no mortgages on my credit report. I have never had a mortgage in my name. My husband and I purposely kept our debt separate. When we got married, our rationale at the time was not to tie up both our credit and credit reports by combining debt. Besides my credit cards, most of our bills were in his name. I know a lot of couples who combine everything and put both their names on bank accounts, mortgages, and credit cards. They share legal obligations to all debts and financial obligations. But I am so glad we thought enough not to do that. (We will talk more about credit later.)

As I faced all my debt, I was overwhelmed with grief and shame! It was a complete shock to find myself in such a bottomless pit! I couldn't believe that I allowed myself to get into that position. I immediately started thinking about what to do to escape this financial mess. My first thought was, "I need a job." I thought, "I need to go to work to pay these people back their money." Then I thought, "Where am I going to work?" I decided to get back into corporate America. I applied for some positions in my field but had no success. Worry and anxiety began to set in. I knew I had to find a solution. It had reached a point for me that there was more debt than money.

The condition of the United States and the world economy had shed a bright light on my finances. I had been paying close attention to the news reports that the United States government owed trillions of dollars to other countries. It was reported that the U.S. owes money to China, Japan, Brazil, Ireland, Russia, and others. I began to wonder, "Why does the United States of America need to owe other countries any amount of money? We are considered one of the wealthiest nations, upheld as an incredible superpower, and admired by other countries. So why are we borrowing money from others?"

I researched how it came to be that this country needed to borrow from others. I found out that the U.S. accumulated a lot of debt to finance the cost of wars. Congress could not fully fund the war through taxation and consequently borrowed the money from other nations. Now, the U.S. government has created a habit of borrowing money to maintain its spending habits. The U.S. debt continues to climb because our government spends more than its income. The U.S. has not been debt-free since 1835 when President Andrew Jackson fully paid off the national debt.

Other People's Money

While pondering why the U.S. needed to owe others, I turned that same question on myself. I wondered, "How did I get into this predicament? Why do I need to owe anybody? How do I owe $100,000 with no job and no income? I am a child of the Most High God. I have a Father in heaven who created everything and owns everything." It was like a light bulb came on in my spirit. "If my Father God owns everything, and I am His child, why should I be in debt?" The more I thought about it, the more it registered in my spirit that I am the child of a King—the King of kings. So, I asked myself, "What king's kid has to borrow to meet their needs?" Just as a good earthly father cares for his children, God would never leave or forsake His children. He knows everything we need and will never leave one need unmet.

I realized that I was a child of God, but I was living like the world. I was a believer who lacked knowledge of God's ways concerning money. I was using credit cards and credit lines to fund the purchase of things I wanted. Most of my spending was for business purchases. However, I habitually used borrowed money to meet my needs. Like the U.S. government, I spent more than my income for many years. I was living beyond my means.

I was beginning to see something wrong with how the world operated with money. I was advised by those who consider themselves wise financial experts that it was wise to use OPM or "other people's money" to build wealth and keep my money for other things. OPM is defined as money borrowed from people, banks, and other lending institutions by individuals and corporations. OPM can be used to buy anything you need or desire, from homes, cars, or yachts to purchasing clothing, gas, or groceries.

When I started using credit, I only had an American Express card, which had to be paid by the end of every month. Then, I started getting offers from other credit companies. I kept getting offers to apply for more credit cards, so I accepted them. I thought, "Why not?" I was making business moves and investing. I hoped to use this borrowed money to profit or bring in huge returns and then be able to pay the principal amount back. I used credit to start businesses such as a home décor business and to get certified as a wedding planner and a licensed real estate agent. I earned some decent money from pursuing each of these ventures. However, after 13 years of accumulating debt and trying different trades and business opportunities, I was not better off. I was in worse shape financially than when I started.

Here is some risky advice I have heard over the years encouraging me to use other people's money:

1. Use credit. Keep your cash for a rainy day or other things.
2. Use debt to your advantage.
3. Use debt as leverage.
4. There is good debt and bad debt.
5. Debt is used by the wealthy to create prosperity.

That advice made sense to me for many years. But I had accumulated $100,000 of debt trying to build wealth using other people's money. All seemed to be well until the recession hit. Then, suddenly, every dime that I was earning came to a halt. That is when I realized the danger and risk of using other people's money.

Many people have made a lot of money using debt, but depending on borrowed money to prosper is a considerable risk. I received a hefty dose of reality that these "other people" wanted their money back despite my situation! My creditors did not want to hear my story about the bad economy. They did not care that I was suffering losses. Instead, they wanted their money back right then and there!

Paying Crazy Interest

As I began facing the reality of my enormous mess, I realized that I needed some help. So, I turned to a nonprofit debt counseling agency to get a grip on my financial situation and get advice. Even though I was ashamed of my financial state, I figured they would understand and not be judgmental. My debt counselor recommended obtaining copies of my credit reports from the three major credit agencies. She also asked me a question I had not considered in a long time. When I first opened all of my accounts, I paid close attention to such things as the terms and rate of interest. Most of the credit card offers I received by mail were for 1-year "interest-free" accounts. It dawned on me that those offers had long expired.

When I finally looked at the interest rates that I was paying on each account, they were no longer 0%. It was now 10 to 13 years later. Some of my accounts showed 12%, 18%, 24.9%, and one was an astounding 32%. I feel stupid to say this, but I had no idea my rates were this high, and the interest was accruing monthly. If I paid the minimum balance, it would take a lifetime to repay this money! It was overwhelming! I knew that I would probably die in all this debt without a miracle.

Time to Pray

I was worried! I never had to worry about money before the recession. I consider myself exceptionally blessed. I always had what I needed. Even growing up as a child, I didn't lack anything. If I lacked anything, I didn't know anything about it. Even after getting married, I never had to worry about finances. My husband is a great provider. He has always had a great position in corporate America and a few side hustles. But in 2010, things were changing. The recession revealed that we had some serious financial issues. I was now worried about money. But I was spiritual enough to know that worry and fear were not of God: *"For God has not given us a spirit of fear, but of power and of love and of a sound mind"* (2 Timothy 1:7, NKJV).

Deep in my spirit, I knew that what I was facing could not be God's best for me. I knew God would disapprove of my financial situation.

I am a praying woman, but I never prayed about money. My finances were always intact, or so it seemed. One day, after receiving another credit card statement in the mail, I knew I could no longer handle this debt; and I did not want to try anymore. It felt like chains were weighing me down. I felt as if I would suffocate.

So, I began to pray.

When I think about it, prayer should have been the first place I turned. But now I was desperate, and my back was against the wall. I did not know what else to do. I needed a Word from the Lord. I remember asking Him, "God, show me where I went wrong." I needed God to show me the truth, even if it hurt. I asked Him to please show me where I erred and got off the right path. I said, "Lord, I want to be free because I do not feel free." I needed peace because I had no peace. I knew God's Word said that if I keep my mind on Him, He will keep me in perfect peace (Isaiah 26:3). I cried out to God like I never had before. I was desperate for His help, guidance, and loving presence.

After pouring my heart out to God for what felt like hours, I settled down enough to hear His still, small voice. I had to shut out all other voices and thoughts in my mind. I had to "take captive" everything I learned from the world that did not line up with the Word—that it was "okay to have debt," "everybody's doing it, and "use other people's money." I focused only on the Lord, believing He would give me peace. I sat on the lounge chair near my bed and prayed, meditated, and intently listened for God to speak. I had listened to the world for so long concerning my finances. Now, I needed to hear from God.

Sitting there, I heard Him say, "Open your Bible to read, and start from the beginning." My Bible was beside me. I opened it to Genesis Chapter 1 and began to read. Almost immediately, it felt like scales were falling from my eyes. I saw words in the Bible that I did not recall seeing before. God was opening my eyes to the truth in His Word. As I was reading, the words on the page spoke to me like never before.

The Truth Will Set You Free

Jesus said, *"If you abide in my word, you are truly my disciples, and you will know the truth, and the truth will set you free"* (John 8:31-32, ESV). I asked God to open my eyes to see the truth. I was ready. I was hungry and thirsty for solutions. So, I began to study God's Word, searching for direction regarding money and debt. I needed to renew my mind to God's will concerning my finances. I needed to gain knowledge of the truth. But I could call on God, and He would show me things I did not know (Jeremiah 33:3).

When God directed me to start studying the Bible in the book of Genesis, I realized He was opening my eyes to how He desired His people to live from the beginning. Reading the book of Genesis revealed that we were created to live a carefree life with God as our sustainer and provider. I could see that before God created man, He provided everything we needed. As I focused on the Garden of Eden, it was clear that God made it, decorated it, and supplied it with everything necessary for survival—air, sunshine, rivers, herbs, and every green plant for food. It was well stocked with man's everyday necessities. God waited to create Adam and Eve last after He provided everything they would need because God is a provider. He made the earth and supplied it with resources to support everything we need to be fruitful and multiply. We do not have to depend on our ability to meet our needs. He took care of everything in advance.

God had given Adam and Eve everything they needed to be happy and fulfilled. He gave them total dominion over everything He created, including the fish of the sea, the birds of the air, the animals, and every creeping thing on the earth. God created everything and then gave man authority over it. God told Adam that there was one thing he could not have: They could not eat from the tree of the knowledge of good and evil. God said to them that if they ate of it, they would surely die (Genesis 2:17).

Instead of believing and obeying God's command, Eve allowed herself to be duped, tricked, and deceived by Satan's lies. The Bible says that Satan is the father of lies, and there is no truth in him (John 8:44). Satan will do all he can to cast doubt on the truth and cause people to disbelieve what God has said and have no faith in the truth.

My blind eyes were opened.

By the time I finished reading the book of Genesis, I had realized how prone human beings were to believe and follow lies. Satan's mission is to keep us blind and stupid—forever. He is our adversary, walking about like a roaring lion seeking whom he may devour (1 Peter 5:8). The Bible tells us that without awareness, the whole world follows the prince of the power of the air (Ephesians 2:2). The devil wants you to be stressed about things outside of your control so that you don't rely on the Lord, the One who gives you strength. The enemy will do everything he can to make you doubt God and His power to provide for you. He wants you to be confused, anxious, or even angry about your life circumstances so that you will eventually become distant from God and rely on your own understanding and efforts to provide for yourself.

Chapter 2

I Was Blind, but Now I See

I HAVE ALWAYS FOUND SOLACE IN READING THE bible, but little did I know how much I was missing until I humbly asked God to reveal the truth. We often approach the Scriptures with preconceived notions, selectively focusing on words that align with our thoughts, thereby closing our eyes to the illuminating truth. Yet, the Word of God is a radiant light that exposes the darkness and wickedness of the world. As children of light, we can examine the Scriptures, uncover the truth, and see the world as it truly is.

My desperation to understand God's perspective on money drove me to delve deeper into the Scriptures. The more I searched, the more I realized I had overlooked key passages about money, debt, and stewardship. I had a startling realization that I was spiritually blind regarding money. Like many Christians today, I had unknowingly assimilated into a worldly society, conforming to its standards and ideals, especially regarding finances. I had wholeheartedly embraced the world's perspective simply because I had not been taught the biblical principles of handling money—not at home, school, or church.

Despite considering myself to be a spiritual person who is dedicated to prayer and Bible study, I did not know what the Bible says about money besides what it says about tithes and offerings. It was a revelation to learn that the Bible not only provides warnings about debt but also outlines potential consequences of indebtedness. The Bible emphasizes that debt can lead to losing freedom and control over one's resources. Numerous verses highlight guidance and principles regarding how Christians should handle financial matters. Those who follow Christ are encouraged to manage their resources wisely, responsibly, and with compassion for others.

I needed to learn what the Scriptures said about money and debt. I had no clue that the Bible warns us to keep out of debt until my back was against the wall and I didn't have enough money to pay my bills. The recession and lousy economy shined a light on my financial situation. I was in big financial trouble and filled with anxiety and fear. But deep down, I knew something was wrong with how I was handling my finances. As a child of God, I knew I should have no fear. I knew that God loved me, and there was no way I should be in a place of lack or desperation. I had nowhere else to turn except to my Father in heaven. I finally realized that the answers I needed lay within the pages of God's Word.

Renewing My Mind

I got saved at the age of 19, and from that time, I was "on fire" for the Lord. I wore almost every "hat" you can think of while serving in the church. I served as a board member, an adult Sunday School teacher, a youth Bible study teacher, a praise team member, a choir member, a small group leader, an evangelist, and more. In 2004, I started teaching and preaching the Gospel in front of congregations. In 2007, I was officially licensed to preach. I was doing everything I thought a good Christian should do to serve God. I went to church every Sunday, every Wednesday for Bible study, every other Thursday for rehearsals, and sometimes on Fridays and Saturdays for special events. Despite all this teaching, preaching, and hearing the Word preached regularly, I found myself in a pit of debt. I was busy and actively serving God in all the ways I knew, but I was missing something: Godly principles to manage my money! After tithing, I had no idea how to handle the other 90% in a way that pleases God.

After being saved, I changed my life in many areas, but not my finances. I was a tither and a giver, but I didn't realize that I needed to surrender 100% of my finances to the Lord and manage all of it with biblical wisdom. Everything I knew about handling money came from the world. I spent many years of my life learning from the world how to make moves with money using credit. I lacked knowledge of the Scriptures and found myself following the patterns of this world concerning money. But 1 John 2:16-17 (NLT) says, *"For the world offers only a craving for physical pleasure, a craving for everything we see, and pride in our achievements and possessions. These are not from the Father but are from this world. And this world is fading away, along with everything that people crave. But anyone who does what pleases God will live forever."*

I needed to renew my mind. I knew that God was not against me having money. I just needed to have my priorities in the right place. It was time to rethink everything I learned from the world. The Bible says in Romans 12:2, *"Do not conform to the pattern of this world, but be transformed by the renewing of your mind. Then you will be able to test and approve what God's will is—his good, pleasing and perfect will."* The pattern of this world belongs to Satan, and it has been ever since Eve fell to temptation. It is a pattern that is contrary to God. But as a born-again believer and follower of Jesus, I can live higher because God's will and His ways are higher. The only way to know God's will is to seek Him and study His Word. God's Word transforms you into a new person by changing your mind. When you change your thinking, you can change your life.

I was ready to change my life because my finances were a mess. I needed the knowledge of God's will, His truth, and His perspective on money and debt. So, I rearranged my priorities. I stopped all my extracurricular activities to focus on God's Word without distractions. I removed all my church "hats" and eliminated most of my church activities except attending Sunday service and teaching youth Bible study. When I was no longer busy doing what I thought was "spiritual," I could prioritize the Word.

I Could See Clearly

As I sought God out, I started to see what it meant to be called out from the world. As a believer, I am called to be a light in this world. Believers cannot affect change in the world and bring light into the darkness if we are a part of that darkness. We must allow the Word of God to become a lamp to our feet and a light to our path. Then we can shine bright for the world to see. People who are lost or in trouble should be able to turn to believers for godly wisdom and direction. But many Christians struggle financially, experiencing foreclosures, evictions, car repossessions, wage garnishment, and debt-collection lawsuits just like the world. We can't help anybody or advance the kingdom because many of us need help.

As I studied the Word for wisdom and revelation, I came across a well-known story of the children of Israel's journey out of Egypt through the Red Sea. I had read this story many times before, but my spiritual eyes were open this time. There was more to this story than I ever saw. The story can be found in the first chapter of Exodus. It is the account of the children of Israel, Pharaoh, and the opening of the Red Sea. Pharaoh and the Egyptians ruthlessly oppressed the Israelites by forcing them into hard labor. The Egyptians made them serve under harsh conditions, making bricks and mortar and working in the fields (Exodus 1:11-14). The Egyptians also placed taskmasters over the Israelites to wear them down with crushing labor and to ensure they performed their daily tasks. Life was so bad for the Israelites that they cried out to God for help, and God heard their cry. God sent Moses as a leader and spokesman to deliver His people from their burdens and the forced labor under Pharaoh.

One day, Moses tells Pharaoh to let the Israelites take three days off to worship and offer sacrifices to God (Exodus 3:18). However, Pharaoh refused to let them go. Pharaoh got so upset because Moses had the audacity to ask that they take three days away from their work. Instead of letting them go, he put more hard work on them that same day. Pharaoh's response was, "No! Get back to your burdens. Get back to work!"

Exodus 5:6-14 (NKJV) says this:
"So the same day Pharaoh commanded the taskmasters of the people and their officers, saying, 'You shall no longer give the people straw to make brick as before. Let them go and gather straw for themselves. And you shall lay on them the quota of bricks which they made before. You shall not reduce

it. For they are idle; therefore, they cry out, saying, Let us go and sacrifice to our God. Let more work be laid on the men, that they may labor in it, and let them not regard false words.'

And the taskmasters of the people and their officers went out and spoke to the people, saying, 'Thus says Pharaoh: I will not give you straw. Go, get yourselves straw where you can find it; yet none of your work will be reduced.' So the people were scattered abroad throughout all the land of Egypt to gather stubble instead of straw. And the taskmasters forced them to hurry, saying, 'Fulfill your work, your daily quota, as when there was straw.' Also, the officers of the children of Israel, whom Pharaoh's taskmasters had set over them, were beaten and were asked, 'Why have you not fulfilled your task in making brick both yesterday and today, as before?'"

As I continued to read, it hit me!

My creditors were like a Pharaoh or master, and I was being lorded over. The Israelites were bonded to their taskmasters, and I was bonded to Visa and *MasterCard*. The Israelites had to work all the time, and everything went to Pharaoh because he provided their needs. I was in the same predicament. I needed to go to work to pay my creditors back. I thought about many of my Christian friends working jobs they hated but couldn't quit because they didn't want to lose their house, car, or all the stuff they had accumulated through loans and credit. They had mortgages to pay, car notes, credit card bills, and student loan debt. I thought about how I was using American Express, Visa, and MasterCard to fulfill my needs. But then, I owed them my time, energy, labor, and money.

While the Israelites were in Egypt, their day was filled with rigorous work from sunup until sundown. They were enslaved people under the affliction of brutal masters. They did not have time to pray or seek God. The only thing they could do was cry out to God. My eyes were open to see that this is what Satan tries to do: Keep you so busy working and meeting your needs that you do not have time to consider the things of God. He wants you to be so distracted about many aspects of life that you will not read or study your Bible as you should. Satan has an agenda, and it is to keep us blind to the truth.

The people of God could not get time off work to worship. Instead of letting them go, Pharaoh calls them "idle" and puts more work on them than before. He did not want them to have time to think about anything except their tasks.

Debt Is Slavery

It hit me like a ton of bricks (no pun toward the brick-making Israelites intended) that I was in debt slavery! My creditors were my taskmasters or slave masters. As I continued to study the subject of slavery, and I began to cross-reference to other books of the Bible, I could see that debt is bondage. It puts people in a place of servitude and oppression to the creditor. The Word says in Proverbs 22:7: *"The rich rule over the poor, and the borrower is a slave to the lender."*

My eyes opened to the fact that rich lenders ruled over me. I had never thought about it like that before. The truth was that lenders and credit card companies did not force me into this bondage. I put myself in that position every time I signed a credit application. I broke down the facts like this: I wanted material things. I wanted to start a business so that I could build wealth. I was going to the rich asking for their money (filling out credit applications). They gave it to me in the form of credit cards and lines of credit. After I spent the money (swiped the cards they gave me), I later owed the money back, with interest. Now, "I owe. I owe. I owe. So, off to work I go." I owed them my future time, labor, and money because they wanted their money back. I understood that a person who feels the need to borrow puts themselves in a position of inferiority to the lender.

I remember it like it was yesterday—when I realized I was a slave. I believe in the Bible. The Bible says that a "borrower is a slave to the lender." And I was a borrower, so I was a slave. I remember saying it over and over out loud, "I'm a slave. I'm a slave. I'm a slave!" I didn't say it proudly. I was upset and hurt and mad. I was ashamed that I was a Christian, an evangelist, and a teacher of the Gospel in this situation. I was disappointed that I had been studying the Word consistently for many years. However, I had not seen this in the Bible before. I was upset that I had been in the church all these years and never even heard Scriptures or anything about debt ever preached by my pastor.

I turned my annoyance briefly to pastors because I had been in church most of my life and never heard a pastor preach about money or debt—only tithing and giving. How could I sit in church two, sometimes three, days a week for over 30 years and never hear a word about God's views towards such an important subject as money?

We need money for almost every aspect of our lives. It is vital that the people of God, disciples of Christ, understand God's view about how we earn, spend, lend, or borrow money. But I had not heard one word of warning from any man or woman of God about debt. Then as I looked around, I noticed that most church leaders, preachers, and pastors were in debt too. They also had big house mortgages, massive church mortgages, substantial car payments, and other debt obligations. They were in the dark about this subject as well. So, I had to take my focus off them. I knew I couldn't play the blame game anyway. I had to continue focusing on getting wisdom and hearing from God on how I would get out of my pit—I was a debt slave.

As an African American woman whose ancestors endured hundreds of years of oppression, bondage, and hard labor, I found it horrifying, disturbing, and offensive to see myself in servitude to any man. When I think about an enslaved person, I think of someone considered to be less than human. An enslaved person was a living tool. Slaves did not have any time that was their own. Their time and energy belonged to the master. A slave had no rights and was at her master's disposal. Her master could beat her, sell her, give her away, and even kill her. Slave owners used free slave labor to build their businesses, build their homes, and create personal economic prosperity. Enslaved people helped to make their masters rich.

When I think back on the slavery of my people, I always wonder how they did it. Why did they stay in such demeaning and oppressive circumstances? I don't believe I could have survived slavery. I would have consistently tried my best to escape. As I thought about this, reality set in. No, I did not have to endure the slavery of the past like my ancestors. But I was in modern-day debt slavery. I was up to my neck in bills, and my creditors demanded their money back. If I did not pay them back, they could call me—making demands. They could garnish my wages (if I had some), and file lawsuits against me. They could also send negative information to the credit bureaus. They had a right to pursue payment for the charges I made.

I'm Nobody's Slave

The more I thought about slavery and my debt, the angrier I got, and I declared, *"I'M NOBODY'S SLAVE!"* I will never forget the day in 2010 when I purposed in my heart that I would get out of debt because I refused to be anybody's slave!

As I studied the Scriptures for the truth, scales fell off my eyes. I could clearly see that debt was not God's will for my life. And it was blocking my road to real success. Do you remember that catchy song by Jimmy Cliff that started with these words: *"I can see clearly now the rain is gone. I can see all obstacles in my way. Gone are the dark clouds that had me blind. It's gonna be a bright (bright), bright (bright) sunshiny day."*

As I got deeper into my studies, it became apparent that being in debt was a serious financial and spiritual issue. To be in debt was to be a slave and serve other men. Jesus addressed the serious problem of being mastered by money in His Sermon on the Mount in Matthew 6:24. He warned that *"No one can serve two masters; for either he will hate the one and love the other, or else he will be loyal to the one and despise the other. You cannot serve God and mammon"* (NKJV). NO ONE can serve God and mammon *(money)*.

The word "mammon" is translated as money, wealth, and riches. The NIV Bible translates the word "mammon" as money (Luke 16:13). Mammon is the spirit behind money. Money is personified as a living person that can be loved and served just like God. Mammon competes for our love and devotion and tries to compel us to serve it, drawing us away from God. Money is neither good nor evil. But what we do with money or how we handle it can be good or evil.

Debt was causing me to serve money. I had to ask myself, "Do I serve God, or do I serve money? Is money controlling my life, or is God the Lord of my life?" I was deep in debt at that point, and the answer was clear. The Scripture plainly says the borrower is a servant to the lender. And Jesus says: You CAN'T serve God and mammon.

But things were about to change for me. My constant prayer was that God would give me the spirit of wisdom and revelation in the knowledge of Him. And that the eyes of my understanding would be enlightened so that I may know His truth (see Ephesians 1:17-18). The Word says that truth would set me free. I was ready to be free!

Chapter 3

The Truth about Money and Debt

THERE IS MUCH TALK TODAY ABOUT THE NEED for financial literacy. So many people need more understanding of finances, which is why they struggle in all areas of money management, including savings, investing, and debt. Too few people understand compound interest, the difference between assets and liabilities, or how to create or balance a budget. Credit is widely used, but most people need more understanding of how credit works. I have found that highly educated people with high incomes are just as ignorant about finances as less-educated, lower-income people. The lack of biblical financial literacy has left many unprepared for a financial crisis and unable to make wise financial decisions.

Money is used in almost every aspect of life. Managing money properly and effectively is an essential life skill and is especially important for Christians. Christians need to understand our roles as stewards or managers of our possessions. We must manage our resources, considering that God is the true owner of everything. The Bible says, *"The earth is the*

LORD's, *and everything in it"* (Psalm 24:1). So, we must be good stewards of God's money and possessions. We are to manage His blessings, His way, for His glory. Stewardship is not just about money; it involves how we manage our work, time, and all of our resources. As stewards (partners or managers), we work with and under God to accomplish His will.

The Bible says much about our responsibilities as God's money managers. The Bible has over 2,300 verses about God's will concerning money. Many of the parables that Jesus taught His disciples were about money. He used the subject of money to teach spiritual truths and reveal our true priorities. To be effective disciples and followers of Christ, we must imitate His example and walk in His teachings.

The Bible is our financial instruction manual. But sadly, too many Christians have no idea what the Bible says about money, nor do they search the Scriptures for financial instruction. Instead, Christians are more likely to consult their family members, people they respect, or a secular financial book or magazine before seeking the wisdom in the Scriptures, but this is a grave mistake. Sadly, as a result, many in the body of Christ are in financial bondage. An even bigger issue is that many believers do not know they are headed for financial ruin.

In 2021, as this book was being written, a pandemic was plaguing the United States and countries worldwide. Businesses were shut down, and many people were out of work. Millions of people depended on government stimulus checks for money to keep afloat. A pandemic or recession can affect anybody, even the rich. But one thing I learned from the recession of 2008 is that a crisis in the economy has less of an effect on a person who is out of debt.

I believe that God is shouting for our attention in the area of money. He is calling for His people to turn our ears to His voice. The world system is failing. If you open your spiritual eyes and ears, you can see it. We must rethink what we were taught about finances because it is the opposite of what God thinks. As the Bible states, we live in this world, but we are not of this world. We are supposed to be living by a different standard. Christians should be an example of righteous living. However, we are struggling financially, just like everybody else. When there is a recession, unbelievers should be running to us for answers because we are making it through. But that is not the case for most Christians; many live paycheck to paycheck, enduring foreclosure and wage garnishments just like everybody else.

Most believers have a wealth of knowledge about the kingdom of this world and its economy but little knowledge about the kingdom of God. The world economy teaches us to use debt and credit to meet our needs. But that's not God's will. The Scriptures tell us that there is a different way to get your needs met in the kingdom of God. The Bible instructs us in Matthew 6:33 to seek FIRST the kingdom of God and His right way of doing things, and He will add everything we need. So, it's time to diligently seek God for His knowledge, wisdom, and truth about money and debt.

The Curse of Debt

God loves His children and has given us financial wisdom and principles for our benefit. The Lord knows debt will cause stress and other emotional, mental, and physical issues. Money issues are one of the leading causes of divorce, loss of friendships, and broken family relations. When we are in debt, we are slaves to the lender. We lack the freedom to serve God as we should and be cheerful givers. We don't have the freedom to go and do whatever the Lord says to do because we have debt obligations to meet. When we rack up debts, we presume that we will be able to earn enough to repay them in the future; but as I found out, debt and interest are designed to pull you deeper into a hole—making it hard to climb out.

If you read this book this far and are not convinced that debt is not God's will for our lives, maybe the following two Scriptures will help you see things more clearly.

Debt and borrowing are under the curse in the Old Testament. However, the ability to be a lender and not a borrower was one of the rewards for obedience to God:

"If you fully obey the LORD your God and carefully keep all his commands that I am giving you today, the LORD your God will set you high above all the nations of the world. You will experience all these blessings if you obey the LORD your God....The LORD will send rain at the proper time from his rich treasury in the heavens and will bless all the work you do. You will lend to many nations, but you will never need to borrow from them" **(Deuteronomy 28:1-2, 12, NLT).**

On the other hand, the promise for disobedience was that you would not prosper in your ways. The need for debt and borrowing was one of the curses for disobedience:

"But if you refuse to listen to the LORD your God and do not obey all the commands and decrees I am giving you today, all these curses will come and overwhelm you....The foreigners living among you will become stronger and stronger, while you become weaker and weaker. They will lend money to you, but you will not lend to them. They will be the head, and you will be the tail!" **(Deuteronomy 28:15, 43-44, NLT).**

Most Christians are heavily in debt. Like most other people, Christians are burdened with mortgage debt, car loans, credit card payments, student loan debt, payday loan debt, etc. The church has conformed to the world's ways and forgotten the laws of God. Many have taken on the ideas of secular financial advisors and secular intellectuals who do not honor the Word of God. Believers are called to be the light of the world. We are called to be holy, separate, and different. We are to let our light shine before others, that they may see our *good works*, and glorify our Father in heaven (Matthew 5:16). But Christians are going to bankers and creditors, who may be nonbelievers, to borrow money for every one of their needs. Christians give out their personal information, expose their credit report, and jump through hoops to qualify for loan approval. But we are commanded to be the lender, not the borrower—the head and not the tail.

When the world has needs, they should come to us and we should be positioned to help. The only debt we should owe is to love and share the Gospel worldwide. However, we can't focus on the mission if we are saddled in debt bondage.

The Truth about Credit

It became critical for me to educate myself about credit. As I learned about God's view of money and debt, my eyes were opened to the world's financial system. I found the world's system of credit to be astonishing and eye-opening.

Credit is a significant component of today's economy. Credit is the ability to borrow money or access goods and services from a lender with an agreement that you will repay later under agreed-upon terms—most times along with interest and possibly other fees. Credit allows you to repeatedly obtain auto loans, mortgages, student loans, and revolving credit accounts. The lender checks your credit report to determine whether or not to front you the money and whether you can reasonably pay it back. Borrowers give lenders permission to look at their credit and borrowing history so the creditor can decide if they will trust them to repay what they borrow. In addition, they look at your private business to determine if you have repaid your obligations on time, missed any payments, or endured any financial setbacks—such as foreclosures or repossessions.

Your credit report becomes your integrity report or your reputation concerning you as a borrower. Whether you rent an apartment, get insurance, or even find a job, your credit report shines a light on your financial well-being. Credit is essentially a tool for lenders to determine your reputation as a borrower.

I must be honest. I thought that loans and credit were required and a normal part of life. I also believed that the U.S. government ran the credit bureaus and credit scoring. But they are not run by the government. I had yet to learn that Equifax, Transunion, and Experian were privately-owned companies that traded stock on the New York Stock Exchange.

I felt stupid to discover that these companies were started by ordinary men who devised the idea to compile our credit history based on our credit accounts, essentially using our social security numbers. They help banks and other lending institutions determine our creditworthiness by keeping track of our spending and bill-paying habits.

These companies rake in billions of dollars to record and report your information. They make money in several ways. One way is by selling your personal information to lenders. When a lender requests your credit report, the credit bureaus charge a fee. They also make money when creditors want to report your information to the bureaus. And think of this, they charge YOU for YOUR report! However, they must give you one free copy of your report each year by law.

It was interesting to find out that credit card companies, auto loan companies, mortgage companies, department stores, cable companies, etc., do not have to report your payment information to the credit bureaus! The credit bureaus do not own your credit information; your credit or loan file belongs to your creditor alone. A creditor is not required by law to report to the credit bureaus. There is no requirement to report your good or bad credit transactions.

I don't know about you, but I had no clue that credit bureaus were corporations and that they made so much money. Transunion is controlled by the Pritzker family, one of the wealthiest families in the United States. And in 2019, Equifax had a revenue of over 3 billion dollars. These agencies have built billion-dollar corporations because of people's willingness to spend money on credit.

The Almighty Credit Score!

I recall the days when I was proud to have a high credit score. Then, I got wise about the credit score game. I learned that a credit score tells lenders your creditworthiness and whether you will likely repay what you borrow. Credit scores help to power this world's financial system. It was news to me to discover that the FICO score is a fairly new concept. This scoring model was introduced to lenders in 1989 and calculates your credit score by performing a complex analysis of the contents of your credit file. These scores are used today to help 90% of lenders make lending decisions. FICO was founded by William Fair (an engineer) and Earl Isaac (a mathematician). They developed a numeric scoring system (FICO credit score) that helps lenders determine whether YOU are a credit risk.

It's a multi-million-dollar corporation that trades on the New York Stock Exchange! This company also advises collection agencies! And they make you and me pay for our credit score! I don't know about you, but this further encourages me that debt is not for me. The lenders, creditors, and credit reporting agencies who keep my credit and scoring file are rich.

It bothers me now when people brag about their credit scores. People spend much time and energy improving their credit scores to get more credit and loans. But don't be deceived. The credit score is mainly used to help lenders determine if you are "worthy" of a loan and whether to charge you a high or low interest rate. A "good credit" score means that you are a *good borrower*. From a biblical perspective, having a high credit score is no reason to brag. You don't need a good credit rating or a high credit score to be "approved" for God's blessings and provision. As a believer, you are already approved!

In 2 Timothy 2:15, the Apostle Paul encourages us to study the Word, so that we are approved by God. Bible study is essential for growing, maturing, and discovering more about God and His will for our lives and finances. It helps us to distinguish truth from error. We will find that we don't need to borrow to meet our needs. As we study the Bible, the Word of truth, we will know the terms of our blessings and inheritance in Christ.

Discovering all this information about credit and credit companies revealed that borrowing is optional. It's a choice. The credit and loan systems are manmade. And as I studied the Word and the world, I gained all the knowledge I needed to help me understand why God said, *"Owe no man anything but love"* (Romans 13:8). The more education you have about personal finance, the better you will be at making sound financial decisions. But on the other hand, if you don't know the truth about this world's system and how it works, it can destroy you.

Financial Stumbling Blocks

Many Christians suffer financially and experience the same sorrows as nonbelievers because they do not know God's will concerning money. However, the answers are in the Scriptures. The Bible is an excellent source of practical knowledge about the dangers and pitfalls of debt. We can avoid many financial mistakes and failures if we heed the lessons referenced in the Scriptures.

Christians make major financial mistakes that cause them to stumble when they abandon the wisdom of the Word of God and follow the world's wisdom. The only way to avoid financial stumbling blocks that cause failure and shame is to experience a radical transformation in your belief system about money. The Bible is the best and most reliable source for guidance on money matters. Though the Bible was written thousands of years ago, its financial wisdom is just as relevant today.

For example, did you know this? In Proverbs, the book of wisdom, the Bible warns that co-signing a loan or becoming surety for another person's debt is poor judgment, stupid, reckless, and lacks good sense. If you co-sign for a loan, you are legally obligated to repay the loan in full if the other person does not or cannot pay. When you co-sign a loan, you are just as responsible for paying as the other person if they miss any payments. Therefore, co-signing a loan is a biblical "no-no" and is a financial stumbling block. Proverbs 17:18 says that it's stupid to guarantee someone else's loan. And at least five other Proverbs reiterate that co-signing for a loan is a trap and a bad idea.

In Proverbs 6, Solomon, the richest and wisest man in the Bible, says if you have co-signed a loan or guaranteed a debt, you have trapped yourself. Then he advises on how to handle it. First, Solomon says to run as fast as possible and beg to get your name off the loan. He says don't rest or sleep until you have freed yourself. Run like a gazelle (one of the fastest animals in the world) when a hunter is chasing him! Read it for yourself:

"My child, if you have put up security for a friend's debt or agreed to guarantee the debt of a stranger—if you have trapped yourself by your agreement and are caught by what you said—follow my advice and save yourself, for you have placed yourself at your friend's mercy. Now swallow your pride; go and beg to have your name erased. Don't put it off; do it now! Don't rest until you do. Save yourself like a gazelle escaping from a hunter, like a bird fleeing from a net" **(Proverbs 6:1-5, NLT).**

That's how dangerous it is to co-sign a loan! And it's easier to get into a loan than it is to get out of one. The banker asks for a co-signer for a reason. The banker sees the borrower as a credit risk. So, they require another person to guarantee the loan in case the borrower doesn't pay. When you promise to secure someone else's loan, you have more confidence in the person's repayment ability than the lender. The Bible warns not to co-sign because that person may not pay, and you may not be able to pay either. Now you are losing your stuff, too.

Proverbs 22:26-27 says, *"Do not be one who shakes hands in pledge or puts up security for debts; if you lack the means to pay, your very bed will be snatched from under you."*

Solomon warns that you will surely suffer harm when you co-sign a loan. If you think about it, you cannot force someone to make payments once you co-sign their loan. You lose all control over the situation. You can only hope and pray that they will repay the loan.

Many parents are co-signing for their children to get student loans. In my coaching business, I have spoken with many parents who have strained relationships with their adult children because their children can't or won't repay their education loans after the parent has co-signed. Nonpayment of a co-signed loan affects the credit and finances of both parties. The Scriptures warn us to owe no man anything but love (Romans 13:8). Debt hurts and strains our relationship with others and causes us to fall out of love.

Thank goodness, I have never co-signed for anybody to get a loan or credit. Thank goodness! We didn't even know what the Scriptures said about co-signing, but when my husband and I got married, we agreed that we would never put our credit at risk together. So, we never put both our names on mortgages, car loans, lines of credit, credit cards, or anything. I am glad we did it that way because my debt did not affect his credit or financial standing when I got into financial trouble.

Now that I know what the Scriptures say about it, I would never co-sign for anybody to get anything. Why should I put myself at risk? I would never co-sign for my son to get a car loan. I would never co-sign for my daughter to get a student loan. I would never co-sign for my best friend to buy furniture. I would never even co-sign with my husband to get a mortgage!

I would never co-sign for my mother, father, brother, sister, or best friend—nobody!

When you learn right-thinking about money, you must stand on it no matter who or what. When you know the truth, you must walk in it, no matter what. There is no good reason to co-sign for anybody, ever!

God's View of Interest

Buying items today and paying for them in the future comes with a cost called *interest* (the Bible calls it usury). When you pay with interest, you pay for the privilege of borrowing money. Many people carry interest on their debt from month to month and allow it to linger for years without paying it off, and that's what I did. I couldn't get ahead because I was constantly paying interest. I was brainwashed into thinking that using other people's money was wiser than using my own, but using other people's money came with a hefty price because of added interest.

I have read several books and heard a handful of pastors speak about God's desire for His people to live debt-free. However, I have not heard anyone address what the Bible says about charging interest. So, I searched the Scriptures to determine whether it is pleasing in God's sight for His people to borrow money with interest, whether for personal or business use.

As I studied the Word to understand God's will toward money, debt, and interest, it became apparent that whenever the Lord mentions borrowing in the Scriptures, He refers to poor people. However, today, almost everybody borrows— no matter their income—for a house, a car, a business, etc. This world's system promotes debt. But it is a trick of the enemy to keep people in bondage. People are not expected to pay cash or make purchases according to what they can afford; they make purchases based on so-called "affordable" monthly payments. When I thought about it, it shows you lack what you need if you have to borrow money. So, you go to someone else to meet that need. But if you are sufficiently supplied with income, why borrow? I never looked at it that way before. Borrowing and paying interest has become a normal way of life. But as I meditated on the Scriptures, it was apparent that the poor borrow to meet their needs.

God knew that the poor would borrow to meet their needs, so He gave instructions in the Old Testament on how to lend to those in need. He told the Israelites not to harden their hearts or shut their hands to the poor and promised to bless those who gave cheerfully. God does not desire that anyone be poor. Poverty is under the curse. But He cares about people experiencing poverty and commands believers to be generous towards them. Proverbs 22:9 (BSB) says, *"A generous man will be blessed, for he shares his bread with the poor."*

I found in the Old Testament that God strictly forbids lending to the poor with interest (Exodus 22:25). If you think about it, lending to poor people and adding interest enriches the lender at the expense of someone in need. Often, it is interest that makes poor people poorer. Payday lenders are a prime example of unfair lending and fees; they give borrowers a short time to repay and charge extremely high interest rates. Many people find it difficult to pay these loans off and find themselves in a vicious financial cycle by repeatedly returning to the payday lender. Borrowers eventually pay more interest and fees than the original amount they borrowed.

In Nehemiah 5, there was a famine in the land, and the Jews were so distressed that they were mortgaging their lands, vineyards, and properties to get food and pay the king's tax on their fields and vineyards. And in their time of need, the wealthy Jews had no compassion for the poor who took extreme measures to take care of their families. The rich were giving them what they needed, but they were taking advantage of them and charging them usury or interest. Moreover, the poor borrowers complained that they were powerless because their brethren, the Jews, were subjecting them to surrender their fields and even took their children into slavery to work off debts.

Nehemiah heard the outcry of the people and saw how this debt was hurting the people experiencing poverty, and he was outraged. Nehemiah pondered the situation and thought about the laws of God, so Nehemiah called a meeting. He told the rich lenders, *"What you are doing is not right. Shouldn't you walk in the fear of our God?"* (Nehemiah 5:9) He commanded that they give the people back their vineyards, land, and houses and give back the interest they were charging on money and food: *"Give back to them immediately their fields, vineyards, olive groves and houses, and also the interest you are charging them—one percent of the money, grain, new wine and olive oil"* (Nehemiah 5:11).

The wealthy Jews agreed and promised to stop exploiting their brethren and return their property and interest. Nehemiah called for the priests and placed the rich under oath to ensure their commitment. Then Nehemiah shook out the folds in his robe, symbolizing what God would do to the wealthy if they failed to fulfill their promise. Nehemiah was warning them that God would "shake out" or "empty out" the possessions of any rich Jew who failed to keep their promise and continued to exploit and oppress the poor. Proverbs 22:16 (NKJV) says, *"He who oppresses the poor to increase his riches… will surely come to poverty."*

Below are a number of Scriptures that emphasize God's heart towards the charging of interest:

"He does not put out his money at interest, Nor does he take a bribe against the innocent. He who does these things will never be shaken" (Psalm 15:5, NASB).

"If you lend money to my people, to the poor among you, you are not to act as a usurer to him; you shall not charge him interest" **(Exodus 22:25, NASB).**

"Do not take interest or any profit from them, but fear your God, so that they may continue to live among you. You must not lend them money at interest or sell them food at a profit" **(Leviticus 25:36-37).**

"Do not charge a fellow Israelite interest, whether on money or food or anything else that may earn interest. You may charge a foreigner interest, but not a fellow Israelite, so that the LORD *your God may bless you in everything you put your hand to in the land you are entering to possess"* **(Deuteronomy 23:19-20).**

"If you loan money to any of the poor among My people, do not treat them as borrowers and act as their creditors by charging interest. If your neighbor gives his coat to you as collateral, then be sure to give it back before night falls— even if he has not repaid you in full. You see that coat covers his body and may be his only protection against the cold. What do you think he would sleep in? When he calls out for Me, I will hear his cry. I am kind and compassionate as you should be when a fellow Israelite is in need" **(Exodus 22:25-27, VOICE).**

I understand from firsthand experience how debt and added interest robbed me of my financial security. Adding interest to a loan places a person at risk of deep bondage and increases the risk of default. The Lord doesn't want His people under debt obligations owed to one another. God told the Israelites time and time again that He brought them out of Egypt, out of slavery, to give them land and be their God (Leviticus 25:38). God Himself was supplying them sufficiently for their needs. They would never need to borrow from anybody or have anyone lording over them because of debt.

Too often, Christians have conformed to the world and see paying interest as a normal way of life. Instead of going to God when we have needs, we automatically think, "I will just get a loan." But shouldn't we stop to find out what God thinks? Many Christians have become numb to God and don't consider Him regarding our finances. We only sense the danger of debt and interest when we are in a serious predicament and it's too late. The moment people step into debt, they lose their freedom — and paying interest worsens the bondage.

In the past, church leaders understood that the Old Testament banned the charging of interest on loans. Somehow, as time progressed, leaders relaxed their stance on whether Christians should pay interest and stopped viewing it as a sin. Christians have conformed to the world's ways and shown no fear of the Lord. Many have tried to redefine what God says about interest to suit their interests and desires. To condone the charging of interest, some people describe usury only as the charging of exceedingly high interest rates. But it is evident in the Word that God prohibited His people from charging one another ANY interest—not on food or anything. They could lend to those in need but without usury or added interest. Jews were allowed to charge interest to foreigners or Gentiles but not to one another.

Clearly, God's people were not to pay interest or be loaned money with interest. One Scripture called it an abomination to lend money with interest and take profit or increase from the poor. When I saw God's heart toward interest and considered how my debt had ballooned out of control, I decided I would never pay interest again. I found God's view on interest clear and profound. Those who charged interest had forgotten God and put their blessings and their very lives in jeopardy:

"'In you they have taken bribes to shed blood; you have taken interest and profits, and you have injured your neighbors for gain by oppression, and you have forgotten Me,' declares the Lord GOD" **(Ezekiel 22:12, NASB).**

"You may charge interest to a foreigner, but to your countrymen, you shall not charge interest, so that the LORD your God may bless you in all that you undertake in the land which you are about to enter to possess" **(Deuteronomy 23:20, NASB).**

"He lends money on interest and takes increase; will he live? He will not live! He has committed all these abominations; he will surely be put to death; his blood will be on his own head" **(Ezekiel 18:13, NASB).**

God's view concerning paying interest is as important for us today as it was for those in ancient Israel. God has not changed. According to His Word, to take interest from a believer who needs to borrow money is to oppress and injure them. It is an unjust gain. It is an abomination. To take added interest from a poor brother or sister is to forget God. To receive interest or collateral from one of God's people is to lack compassion.

I received no mercy from my creditors when I was $100,000 in debt, and most of the debt was added interest! None of my creditors cared about what I was going through. They just wanted their money back.

But I will say this: Interest is the price you pay for going to man instead of God to meet your needs. And interest is the price paid for materialism and borrowing to get things you can't afford. There was a price to pay for our sins, and Jesus Christ paid that price for us. He who knew no sin gave His life for us so that we can live and have an abundant life.

Chapter 4

The Blessing Is Enough

A S I CONTINUED STUDYING, I LEARNED THAT I
was not to consider myself the owner of any of my
money or possessions. God owns it all. The Bible says, *"The
earth and everything in it, the world and its inhabitants, belong to
the LORD"* (Psalm 24:1, HCSB). Money does not belong to
you or me. It belongs to God. We are here to be stewards or
managers of what He has given. A steward is a person who
manages things that belong to someone else.

Jesus provides us with a view of what good and bad
financial stewardship look like in the Parable of the Talents
in Matthew 25. This short story is about a master and his
three servants. We learn from this parable that the master
entrusted three of his servants with a certain amount of
wealth. He gave a certain amount to each of them according
to their ability. The master goes away but returns to settle
accounts with them and see whether they were faithful over
what they were given. The master commended the two
servants who gained more wealth. The one steward who
didn't invest or earn more money was scolded and called

wicked. It was this parable that made me realize that being in debt was wicked. God had blessed me with income, but I entangled it with debt and blew it. I was trying to make my money grow, but I was doing it the world's way.

Debt and interest payments were eating up all my increases. I knew I was supposed to be blessed, but I was trying to "get blessed" in my own strength. I was using debt and credit to start businesses and to build wealth. I thought I was doing the right thing by trying to make money. I figured I wouldn't have to worry about my future and could give more and help more people. But I found myself in bondage and a slave to my money. God was no longer the master of my life; I had 11 other masters (Visa, MasterCard, Citibank, Providian, American Express, etc.). I had no idea what the Word of God said about debt. I was not purposefully in debt; I was ignorantly in debt. But when I found the Scripture that said to owe no man nothing but love (Romans 13:8), I could not ignore God's will concerning debt. I knew that I could not be on both sides of the fence. I could not be for debt and against debt. I either wanted to please God or the world.

There was no way I could give my total allegiance to both God and money. Thoughts about my debts consumed my mind day in and day out. Instead of focusing on God, I spent most of my thoughts trying to figure out would do and how I would pay my creditors back. Debt was ruling and ruining my life.

Financial Idols Must Be Cast Down

The nature of God is that He will not tolerate our mixed devotion. He expects our whole hearts and minds to be focused on Him. He loves us and is sure to provide for us. But we're always so busy chasing after things and the world's empty pleasures that we never fully experience the fullness of His love and provision. The world is full of distractions, and the enemy is strategic in his plans to get us to serve our idols rather than God. When thinking about the word "idol," we often think of statues and objects that were worshiped by pagans in ancient cultures. However, the idols of today are anything that takes God's place in our hearts—such as careers, relationships, hobbies, entertainment, sports, goals, addictions, greed, prestige, money, or possessions.

The goal of the enemy is for us to run to him when we need something. But Jesus says, *"You cannot serve two masters; you cannot serve God and money"* (Matthew 6:24). We cannot have two providers or serve two masters. I cannot say I trust God to provide all my needs, but then I go to the world asking for loans and credit to meet my needs. I could see that my creditors were like idols or other gods. Whenever I had needs or desires or wanted to start a business, I turned to credit cards and lines of credit. I never acknowledged God in what I was doing or asked Him to provide. I thought of God as my provider, but American Express, MasterCard, Visa, Citibank, and others were my real providers. I did not realize it, but they were my substitute gods.

As I read the Scriptures, I remembered that one of the Ten Commandments prohibits having other gods. Exodus 20:2-5 says, *"I am the LORD your God, who brought you out of Egypt, out of the land of slavery. You shall have no other gods before me. You shall not make for yourself an image in the form of anything in heaven above or on the earth beneath or in the waters below. You shall not bow down to them or worship them; for I, the LORD your God, am a jealous God."*

It may seem ridiculous to think that we might be worshipping idols made of silver, gold, dollar bills, or plastic credit cards. But Psalm 115:4 (BSB) says exactly what men worship: *"Their idols are silver and gold, made by the hands of men."* As I contemplated this Scripture, I thought about the Israelites and how God rescued and redeemed them from the slavery of Pharaoh and the Egyptians by providing them a way out through the Red Sea. Not long after they were led to freedom on the other side of the sea, they created for themselves something to worship—a god made of gold in the form of a calf. The gold they used to make their god was the gold the true God gave them. It was the wealth God allowed them to take from their oppressors.

As the story goes, before they left Egypt, God told the Israelite women to ask their Egyptian neighbors and foreign women for their gold and fine articles of clothing. The people did not know that the Israelites would leave town with all these goods. But God made sure that they would not leave Egypt empty-handed. Not only did God free them from slavery, but He also made sure they would not lack anything when they got out of Egyptian bondage. The story of the Israelites' journey to freedom reassured me that I would not have to live in poverty or worry about how I would survive when I got out of debt bondage.

I looked closely at how God cared for His people who were coming out of oppression. Pharaoh had been taking care of their essential needs. But they would need Pharaoh no more. God knew they would need provisions, so He showed the Israelites favor and gave them the wealth of their oppressors. God told them, *"And I will cause the Egyptians to look favorably on you. They will give you gifts when you go, so you will not leave empty-handed. Every Israelite woman will ask for articles of silver and gold and fine clothing from her Egyptian neighbors and from the foreign women in their houses. You will dress your sons and daughters with these, stripping the*

Egyptians of their wealth" (Exodus 3:21-22). God allowed them to strip their enemies of all their wealth. All they had to do was receive it. This account increased my faith that God would get me out of my debt bondage AND supply all my needs!

By this point in my studies, I had a strong desire to get out of debt. I could see that God has more than one way to bless His people. God is always faithful in doing His part. But we must trust Him and follow His guidance. I was learning through the journey of the Israelites that obedience has been the problem. When I went off in my direction—as I did with debt and loans—it brought suffering. But if I do things God's way and keep out of debt, God will bless me.

As I continued to study the Scriptures, I realized how important it was to keep my eyes on God so that I wouldn't be tempted to turn back to the misery of debt, thinking it was easier than trusting God. I paid close attention to the Israelites' journey as they exited Egypt through the Red Sea. Even though their former captors pursued them to bring them back into slavery, God destroyed them. God allowed the children of Israel to pass safely through the sea, but their enemies who chased behind them didn't survive. *"And when the Israelites saw the great power the LORD displayed against the Egyptians, the people feared the LORD and trusted him and Moses his servant"* (Exodus 14:31).

The Israelites witnessed God's great power and how He saved them. But a mere two months and fifteen days after they were rescued from the misery they endured in Egypt, the Israelites were already grumbling and complaining about what they were going to eat. They complained to their leaders—Moses and his brother Aaron—that they would starve and die of thirst in the wilderness. They wished they were back in Egypt, where they had more than enough to eat: *"In the desert, the whole community grumbled against Moses and Aaron. The Israelites said to them, 'If only we had died by the LORD's hand in Egypt! There we sat around pots of meat and ate all the food we wanted, but you have brought us out into this desert to starve this entire assembly to death'"* (Exodus 16:2-3). Then they complained because they wanted something to drink: *"Why did you bring us up out of Egypt to make us and our children and livestock die of thirst?"* (Exodus 17:3b)

Moses was sent to lead them out of cruel and hard labor; and they were free, but they showed no gratitude. Instead, they complained. It was evident that the Israelites did not trust God or the leader that God gave them. They were so discouraged that they wanted to go back to the hard life they had been living.

Imagine this: While in Egypt, they cried out for God to help them; and God rescued them. Now, they needed food and water, and acted like God couldn't do that, too. They had soon forgotten all the mighty acts God had demonstrated against Pharaoh. They didn't remember how the Lord opened the Red Sea before their very eyes and destroyed their enemies. Their reaction to the pressure they were facing was to head back to Egypt.

The Land of Plenty

The Israelites had forgotten how faithful God had been to them all along. He promised them if they obeyed Him and kept His covenant, He would make them His treasured possessions, kings, and priests (see Exodus 19:5-6). He promised to bring them up from Egypt and take them to the Promised Land—a good and large land flowing with milk and honey where there would be plenty and no lack. They were on the journey of a lifetime. They were headed toward more than enough. But they could not see past what was right in front of them. They were stubborn, hard-hearted, and had no faith. They were headed toward God's best, but were so faithless that they couldn't endure the tests and trials along the way.

The Israelites had been saved from bondage and were led into the wilderness, away from the world and all the influences. They probably thought life would be easy from now on. But they had some lessons to learn. They were being called out and set apart from all the pulls of society. The wilderness had a divine purpose. It was a place of testing and trial, where they could develop humility and perseverance and learn to fully rely on God to provide. They needed to learn to trust God for everything. They were not alone in the wilderness; God was there sustaining them. He knew exactly what they needed and when they needed it. God supernaturally led them with a cloud by day and fire by night. He fed them food from heaven, called "manna." But they kept wanting something more.

The Israelites had come out of Egypt, but Egypt was still very much in them. They were physically free but still carried the carnal mindset of Egyptian life. They still had the "world" tugging at their hearts. However, separating from the world is a crucial requirement as disciples of Christ. God clearly tells us to "Come out from among them and be separate" (2 Corinthians 6:17). But they were being pulled back into compromise, human reasoning, societal pressure, and the lure of convenience. They were filled with worry about life and getting their needs met. They got their eyes off God and desired to turn back to their old life, even if that life was filled with bondage.

It was clear that things go very wrong when we get off God's path and try to figure things out for ourselves. We somehow think we have a better way or a better plan. Jesus revealed that worry about life and getting our needs met pull us away from dependence on Him. The tendency to worry about the necessities of life leads people to run after money and get it any way they can, including using debt and loans. Ultimately, the result of worry is bondage.

Jesus says in Matthew 6:24-27:
"No one can serve two masters. Either you will hate the one and love the other, or you will be devoted to the one and despise the other. You cannot serve both God and money.

Therefore I tell you, do not worry about your life, what you will eat or drink; or about your body, what you will wear. Is not life more than food, and the body more than clothes? Look at the birds of the air; they do not sow or reap or store away in barns, and yet your heavenly Father feeds them. Are you not much more valuable than they? Can any one of you, by worrying, add a single hour to your life?"

Jesus said that there was no reason to worry about your life. Life is more than food and clothes. When you look around, not even the birds worry about where they will get food. If our heavenly Father provides for them, what more will He do for His dear children? God is more than capable of providing for a person whom He created in His image. Are you not more valuable to God than a bird?

One day I watched a bird gather straw and other items to build a nest. It would fly away and fly back to the nest with building materials. The bird didn't have any worries. It did not need to go to a bird bank to borrow money to buy anything to build its home. It just went out and gathered what the Father had already provided. If God provides for the birds of the sky, He will take care of you and me who are His special creation, made in His likeness.

What is the use of worrying? What will it help or change? Worry does not bring food, clothes, shelter, or money. Worrying is the opposite of having faith.

"And why do you worry about clothes? See how the flowers of the field grow. They do not labor or spin. Yet I tell you that not even Solomon in all his splendor was dressed like one of these. If that is how God clothes the grass of the field, which is here today and tomorrow is thrown into the fire, will he not much more clothe you—you of little faith?" **(Matthew 6:28-30)**

Jesus asks, "Why do you worry about clothes?" If God clothes the grass of the field with beautiful flowers, how much better will He dress you in fine raiment? God created our bodies. We were made in His image. Jesus mentions King Solomon, who lived in great wealth and luxury. But even Solomon was not dressed as fine as a field of grass. If our Father in heaven clothes the grass, He will make sure you have fine clothes too. The grass is here today and gone tomorrow. But God has given you eternal life.

"So do not worry, saying, 'What shall we eat?' or 'What shall we drink?' or 'What shall we wear?' For the pagans run after all these things, and your heavenly Father knows that you need them. But seek first his kingdom and his righteousness, and all these things will be given to you as well" **(Matthew 6:31-33)**.

Living by Faith

In Matthew 6:30, Jesus said four words that stood out in my spirit: *"You of little faith."* In other words, "Why are you so afraid?" and "Why do you doubt?" I thought, "That's it." We worry and don't trust our heavenly Father to provide because we have "little faith." Anxiety will rule our daily lives if we don't build our faith in God. Faith comes by hearing the Word of God. We build our faith as we *seek after* God and His righteous ways. God promised that if we search for Him, we will find Him (Deuteronomy 4:29). He is not playing hard to get.

I had not been taught the truth about God's promise to provide everything I needed. I didn't hear any preacher teach specifically to have faith in God for my daily needs. I was taught that going to college and getting a good job was the answer to that. The world taught me to use other people's money—credit, debt, and loans—to achieve my goals.

I had faith in God as Savior, healer, and protector. But I didn't know God as Jehovah Jireh, my provider. As I studied, I found that it is God's will and good pleasure to provide for me. Like any good parent, He provides for His children who trust Him. In the Lord's Prayer, Jesus teaches His followers to ask for provision. We declare our daily dependence on God when we pray, *"Give us today our daily bread"* (Matthew 6:11). God desires a relationship with us, which involves trusting and depending on Him to meet our daily requirements.

Jesus tells us that pagans and nonbelievers must run after money because they are without God and His promises. People without faith anxiously worry about how to get what they need. But as a born-again believer, I don't have to struggle and toil to meet my needs.

Jesus gives us the answer to worry about life! He says, *"Seek first the kingdom of God and His righteousness, and all these things will be given to you as well."* Our priority in life should be to pursue God, and when you do this, *"all things"* you need—food, drink, clothes, housing, blessings, wealth, favor, protection, peace, joy, etc. — will be given to you. These things come from God as a by-product of seeking Him.

I saw the word "given" and thought, "My Father wants to *give me* what I need." I had to stop seeking wealth and material possessions and put all my effort into seeking God. Proverbs 21:21 says, *"Whoever pursues righteousness and love finds life, prosperity and honor."* When you seek Him, you will find the right way to live this life and won't have to beg or borrow to get anything. If God gave us His only Son, what more will He give us? *"He who did not spare his own Son, but gave him up for us all — how will he not also, along with him, graciously give us all things?"* (Romans 8:32)

Heirs Don't Need Debt!

As I meditated on this verse from Romans 8:32, I began to rejoice because I knew that I did not have to worry about getting my needs met ever again. No matter what I need, my Father God will provide. He did not withhold His very best from me and gave me His Son, Jesus. Why would He withhold any good thing from me? I recognized that salvation included much more than forgiveness of sins and healing. Salvation included ALL THINGS!

My faith was building.

Everything that belongs to Father God became ours when we were born again. We became children of the King of kings and entered a royal family with a vast fortune. Since we are His children, everything He has belongs to us! As believers, we belong to the One who owns the cattle on a thousand hills, the silver, and the gold. Therefore, we must renew our minds to see ourselves as heirs of God and discover what is included in our inheritance.

Because we are His children, we qualify for all His treasures! John 1:12 (NLT) says, *"But to all who believed him and accepted him, he gave the right to become children of God."* Through God's gracious adoption, we have become His children. *"Now if we are children, then we are heirs—heirs of God and co-heirs with Christ"* (Romans 8:17a). We become heirs by this new birth into God's family. You are God's son or daughter and a sibling with Christ!

When a man is born-again, he is born into a new order of existence and is connected to a divine source, and all needs are met through faith. As born-again believers, you and I no longer need to depend on the world's money system of loans, credit cards, and lines of credit. We have a covenant right to live in sufficiency and free from debt! You are heir to everything you will ever need! Our God-given right as God's children is to live in complete abundance. However, most believers are walking around acting as if they are broke when we are truly rich!

A King's kid does not have to go outside of the kingdom of God for provision. What child of a king needs to go to the bank and sit down with a lender, asking for a loan? What child of a king needs to run up credit card debt? What child of a king needs to go to the world to ask for money to pay for anything? My eyes were opened to the difference between the kingdom of God and the kingdom of the world. No child of the King should be in debt bondage.

Blessed Like Abraham

I found out through studying the Bible that I am blessed like Abraham, who is known as the father of faith. Abraham obeyed God and trusted His promise without knowing how God would make it happen, yet he obeyed anyway. And because of his faith, God approved of Abraham. God's covenant promise with Abraham is remarkable: *"The LORD had said to Abram, 'Go from your country, your people and your father's household to the land I will show you. I will make you into a great nation, and I will bless you; I will make your name great, and you will be a blessing. I will bless those who bless you, and whoever curses you I will curse, and all peoples on earth will be blessed through you'"* (Genesis 12:1-3).

Abraham was fully persuaded that God could do what He promised. God promised Abraham that he would have a son and that his descendants would be more numerous than he could count—even though he was old and his wife Sarah was barren. The Bible says, *"Abraham believed the LORD, and he credited it to him as righteousness"* (Genesis 15:6). Abraham believed the promises that God made to him even when his circumstances didn't match what God told him.

In the New Testament, Paul emphasizes that the blessing of Abraham, which was originally given to Abraham and his descendants, extends to all believers—Jew and Gentile— through faith in Jesus Christ. So then, those who are of faith are blessed along with Abraham. The promises and blessings made to Abraham are fulfilled through the work of Christ, and this fulfillment is available to all of us through faith.

Because you belong to Christ, you are Abraham's seed and heirs of God's promise. *"For all of you who were baptized into Christ have clothed yourselves with Christ. There is neither Jew nor Gentile, neither slave nor free, nor is there male and female, for you are all one in Christ Jesus. If you belong to Christ, then you are Abraham's seed, and heirs according to the promise"* (Galatians 3:27-29).

How did Abraham receive what God promised? Abraham believed God. To walk in the blessings of God, you must believe that God will do what He says He will do and declare it with your mouth! The Gospel is about believing! God has not changed. He is still the God of Abraham. He's a promise keeper, a way maker, and He can be trusted. God fulfilled all His promises to Abraham, including blessing him financially. Genesis 13:2 says, *"Abram had become very wealthy in livestock and in silver and gold."*

When you believe God, provision comes along with it. God's Word promises that He will supply all your needs. This blessing and supply includes all your needs—physical, material, and financial. You must believe like Abraham believed and declare what God said!

I made up my mind that whatever I needed, God will freely provide it, or He will bless the work of my hands and increase me financially so that I can buy it. Either way, God supplies. I don't need to run to man for anything. God may use man to bless me. But I don't have to subject myself to the bondage of debt to get my needs met.

Don't Be Deceived

Even though I knew what the Word said about money and debt and the blessed life, the devil still tried to convince me that using credit and loans was the only way to make it. Years after I was out of debt and living in freedom, the devil still came with his arsenal of lies trying to make me believe it wasn't enough. So, it was obvious that the devil was in the details. His goal is to keep our eyes off God and on our needs and desires so that we will run to him.

Satan knows the desires of man. He knows the influence that money has on our lives. Money makes us feel powerful, influential, and secure. If we are not careful, we can easily fall into the trap of running after money. The Bible says, *"For the love of money is the root of all kinds of evil. And some people, craving money, have wandered away from the true faith and pierced themselves with many sorrows"* (1 Timothy 6:10, NLT).

Debt caused me to give up my influence, freedom, and the blessed life. It was equivalent to what Adam and Eve did in the Garden. God blessed them and gave them dominion over everything, but they sold out to the devil, who convinced them that God's way was flawed and unfair. Satan made Eve question God's character and made the corrupt way look better and more glorious.

When Adam and Eve disobeyed and ate from the Tree of the Knowledge of good and evil, they gave Satan legal jurisdiction over the earthly realm. Adam had dominion, but he transferred the power God gave him over to Satan. Then Satan became the god of this world (2 Corinthians 4:4). Adam and Eve gave up their authority. That's what I did with debt. Before I got into debt, I was free. I had dominion. I was the head. But the moment I took money from the world, I became a servant and the tail.

Satan is the master of lies and deception. His job is to make us doubt God. On the one hand, I believed deep down that debt was wrong, but at the same time, I wondered how I would live entirely without it. Then I thought about what happened to Eve. She knew God's command. She knew that the tree of the knowledge of good and evil was off-limits. But she blew it because she wanted more. Satan deceived Eve into thinking that she was missing out on something.

I thought about the voices in my head that wanted to convince me that I didn't understand what God *really meant* when He said, *"Owe no man anything but love."* My mind was analyzing what God meant and whether I shouldn't owe *anybody anything*. By this time, I found a few Christian authors who agreed that debt was not God's best, but they felt it was acceptable to use debt for a mortgage, make investments, and run a business. But that didn't make any sense to me. God meant what He said and said what He meant. The Scriptures are clear and convincing. God does not want His people in bondage to debt!

I thought about the sorrow that came to Eve after she disobeyed God's command in the Garden. She believed Satan's lie when he said to her, *"You will not surely die."* Then he made her question God's motives and His reason for the commandment: *"God knows that your eyes will be opened as soon as you eat it, and you will be like God, knowing both good and evil"* (Genesis 3:4-5, NLT). And poor Eve didn't want to miss out on her opportunity for self-improvement. So, she started thinking with worldly logic instead of being spiritually minded.

Eve began to see things with her own eyes instead of filtering through her spiritual eyes. She decided to do what pleased her instead of God. Eve no longer believed that God had her best interest at heart. So, one day, she looked at the fruit of the tree and saw what she wanted to see. She saw that it was good for food and pleasing to her eyes, and she desired the wisdom it would bring. So, she took some and ate it. She also gave some to Adam, and he ate it, too (Genesis 3:6).

It was clear to me that Satan is a master of deception. Whenever I used Visa and MasterCard, I thought I was doing something good for myself. The glitz and glamour of the world deceived me. When the world promises you provision, they dangle it right in your face and make you feel like you deserve it. I was convinced I could get ahead in life by using credit. But it was the opposite. I was digging a large hole and sinking deeper and deeper into it.

Plus, everybody was in debt. I didn't know one person who wasn't straddled by debt. I wondered how so many people could be in such deception. Then God showed me Scripture after Scripture, revealing that Satan is the god of this world, and his purpose is to deceive the whole world. For instance, 2 Corinthians 4:4 (NLT) says, *"Satan, who is the god of this world, has blinded the minds of those who don't believe. They are unable to see the glorious light of the Good News. They don't understand this message about the glory of Christ, who is the exact likeness of God."*

The Bible says that Satan is a thief and comes only to steal and kill and destroy (John 10:10). He is the god of this world because man turned it all over to him in the Garden. Adam was in the Garden with the gold (Genesis 2:12), but he delivered it over to Satan. Satan admits that the kingdoms of the world were delivered to him. And Satan has the authority to give it to whoever he wants. We can see this when Satan tried to tempt Jesus with worldly wealth and possessions.

Luke 4:5-8 (NKJV) says:
"Then the devil, taking Him up on a high mountain, showed Him all the kingdoms of the world in a moment of time. And the devil said to Him, 'All this authority I will give You, and their glory; for this has been delivered to me, and I give it to whomever I wish. Therefore, if You will worship before me, all will be Yours.'

And Jesus answered and said to him, 'Get behind Me, Satan! For it is written, 'You shall worship the Lord your God, and Him only you shall serve.'"

It is astonishing to think that Satan was bold enough to try to persuade Jesus to serve and worship him. However, Jesus was aware of Satan's tactics. Satan thought he was offering Jesus a great deal when he offered to give Jesus power, control, and glory. But Jesus knew what the Word of God said, and He wouldn't be moved or be swayed away from it by some slick, conniving devil. When Satan spoke, Jesus answered him with the Word of God. Jesus answered,

"It is written: 'Man shall not live on bread alone, but on every word that comes from the mouth of God'" (Matthew 4:4).

Satan is a master of manipulation. That's why it is crucial to know the Word of God to know how to respond to his tactics. Satan lies, and he does it big. When someone tells you a big enough lie, and it sounds good, you may fall for it if you don't know the Scriptures. That's why it is essential to know God's Word and His voice and be committed to following His commands. We must always be alert and have a godly answer in every situation. The Bible warns, *"Be sober, be vigilant; because your adversary the devil walks about like a roaring lion, seeking whom he may devour. Resist him, steadfast in the faith"* (1 Peter 5:8-9, NKJV).

I have decided that it doesn't matter what the world is saying or doing, I trust God. My family, friends, and neighbors may all be using debt and credit to live. But I will abide by the Word of God. I will stand on the promises of God until I see them manifest in my life. His Word cannot fail. If He said it, He must do it. The Lord will bless me as He promised, and I will be the lender and never the borrower because I trust Him.

God Promised to Bless You

The more I studied and reflected on the Scriptures, the more I was convinced I would never need debt again. Two Passages from the book of Deuteronomy sealed the whole debt issue for me. These Passages are part of a larger section known as the blessings and curses, where God outlines the blessings that will come upon the Israelites if they obey His commandments—including staying out of debt—and the curses that would befall them if they turned away from His instructions.

It says in Deuteronomy 28:12-14 (KJV):

"The LORD shall open unto thee his good treasure, the heaven to give the rain unto thy land in his season, and to bless all the work of thine hand: and thou shalt lend unto many nations, and thou shalt not borrow. And the LORD shall make thee the head, and not the tail; and thou shalt be above only, and thou shalt not be beneath; if that thou hearken unto the commandments of the LORD thy God, which I command thee this day, to observe and to do them: And thou shalt not go aside from any of the words which I command thee this day, to the right hand, or to the left, to go after other gods to serve them."

Deuteronomy 15:6 also says, *"For the LORD your God will bless you as he has promised, and you will lend to many nations but will borrow from none. You will rule over many nations but none will rule over you."*

There was no denying what these Scriptures were saying. First of all, the words *"thou shalt not"* stood out. I recalled that these three words were used when God gave Moses the Ten Commandments. These were commands, not suggestions. God was clearly promising to provide them with an open heaven and blessings if they kept His commandments. They were promised financial prosperity so that they would always be lenders and never borrowers. But they must not turn away from God's commandments to worship other gods. Idolatry was strictly prohibited.

As I meditated on these Scriptures, I chewed on every single word. Finally, I saw that God has a way to bless us that no one could. The world wants us to depend on them and borrow, but God wants to bless us with His "good treasures." God wants to open windows and doors for us that no man can shut. He wants to show us favor and provide opportunities that will cause us to be successful.

I realized that I wouldn't have to borrow because God

would bless me as He promised. He will bless all the work of my hands. God wasn't just going to drop money from the sky, even though He could if He wanted to. But if I would be obedient to His Word and help those in need but stay out of debt myself, He would open doors and windows of opportunities that would cause me to be blessed. I would always be the lender, never the borrower!

As I continued to set my eyes on these Scriptures, I saw some words that got my attention. God said in Deuteronomy 28:13 (KJV), *"And the LORD shall make thee the head and not the tail; and thou shalt be above only, and thou shalt not be beneath; if that thou hearken unto the commandments of the LORD thy God."* It was crystal clear that borrowing places you at the bottom. I knew that feeling very well because my credit card debt made me feel like I was in a bottomless pit that I couldn't climb out of. But keeping out of debt and being in the position to lend keeps you on top, which is where every believer should be— at the top and never at the bottom.

The Message version of the Bible best describes what it is like for a person who follows God's commands: *"GOD will throw open the doors of his sky vaults and pour rain on your land on schedule and bless the work you take in hand. You will lend to many nations but you yourself won't have to take out a loan. GOD will make you the head, not the tail; you'll always be the top dog, never the underdog, as you obediently listen to and diligently keep the commands of GOD, your GOD, that I am commanding you today. Don't swerve an inch to the right or left from the words that I command you today by going off following and worshiping other gods"* (Deuteronomy 28:13-14, MSG).

Here, we can see that if God's people were faithful to God's covenant by following God's commands and staying true to their faith, they would be rewarded with prosperity, influence, and blessings. But in contrast, Deuteronomy 28:43-45 (NLT) sheds light on the curses and consequences that will follow disobedience: *"The foreigners living among you will become stronger and stronger, while you become weaker and weaker. They will lend money to you, but you will not lend to them. They will be the head, and you will be the tail!"* This verse warns about the negative spiritual and economic consequences of straying from the path of obedience and faithfulness to God's command. Instead of being leaders or the dominant force, the Israelites would become subservient, symbolized by being "the tail."

This verse magnifies the shift and reversal in economic dynamics. Rather than being in a position of lending and economic strength, they would find themselves in a position of borrowing and financial dependence and reliance on others. Turning away from God's principles would result in a loss of divine favor, loss of authority, less influence, decreased strength, economic decline, a lower social status, and overall deterioration of well-being.

As I meditated on this verse, I could see how important it was to remain in covenant with God and how ugly it was to be in debt to the lender. God began to show me that I signed up to be the tail every time I filled out a credit application. It was as if I could hear God asking me some questions.

My conversation with God went something like this:

> *God:* "Michelle, whose name was at the top of those credit applications that you filled out to get those credit cards?"
>
> *Me:* "Well, the name of the bank or lending institution was at the top."
>
> *God:* "You are correct. Now, whose name was at the bottom of the application?"
>
> *Me:* "I signed my name at the bottom."
>
> *God:* "Now, do you see how you became the tail?"

Then I declared, "That's it. I am *not* going to play the devil's game!" I wanted no part in his money system. I knew I couldn't be on both sides of the fence. Either I'm going to serve God or serve the devil. I wanted out. I wanted to please God. I was ready to be free! I had uncovered more than enough Scriptures that made me want to stop and take a serious inventory of my life.

Time to Repent

I knew it was time to repent. I knew that I was not living the life that Jesus died for me to live. Jesus came that I might have life and have it more abundantly (John 10:10). So, I cried out to God and told Him all that I had done. Proverbs 28:13 says, *"Whoever conceals their sins does not prosper, but the one who confesses and renounces them finds mercy."* I needed His mercy, His grace, and deliverance. I confessed that I did not know His will concerning money. I confessed to God that I had no business running up over $100,000 in debt. I acknowledged to God that I allowed my creditors to supply my needs instead of depending on Him. I confessed that I was a slave and serving money.

When I say repent, I mean I decided to agree with the Word and turned away from living a life of debt and borrowing money to meet my needs. I changed my mind from believing that using other people's money was the way to live. Instead, I accepted the Word of God that says, *"owe no man anything,"* and accepted that God would supply all my needs according to His riches (Romans 13:8; Philippians 4:19).

After I confessed, I was relieved of so much anxiety. I no longer felt the weight of feeling as if I had betrayed God by serving other gods. I knew that God loved me, and nothing could separate me from His love. God is compassionate, gracious, and slow to anger. I trusted that He was no longer holding my transgression against me. I knew that according to 1 John 1:9, if I confess my sins, He is faithful in forgiving my sins and cleansing me of all unrighteousness. I resolved that day that I would never use credit cards to meet my needs again! So, after I confessed my sins and troubles to God, I began to pray. I declared to the Lord that if He would help me get out of debt and set me free, I would never return to debt again.

And you may have made some huge financial mistakes and are struggling. Repent! Turn from those ways that don't agree with your identity as royalty and a co-heir with Christ! It doesn't matter how big or small the debt is. There is nothing too hard for God!

Chapter 5

God Made a Way

I CONTINUED TO STUDY AND SEEK THE WORD OF god day and night. I came up from the Bible long enough to cook, clean, and meet my family's needs. Then, I went right back to it. I woke up in the morning studying the Scriptures. And many times, I fell asleep at night with my Bible because I was so hungry for the Word. I was starving for the truth. I needed spiritual food.

I diligently sought the Lord, and before I knew it, three years had passed. The more I studied, the more I got to know God, and the more I got to know myself because I am made in His image. I did not evolve from some lower form of life. Having God's image means that I should follow His example—imitating His character, love, and selflessness. As an imitator of God and His dear Son, Jesus Christ, I should live a life of goodness and righteousness. I should conduct my life in a manner that reflects my identity and status as God's beloved child. I must live a life worthy of being called a child of God.

I was created by God to have dominion on the earth, to be His ambassador, to be a light, and to bring Him glory in this world. I am on this earth on assignment. I have been called to live in a manner that aligns with God's principles and values. As I focused on God and discovered my identity in Christ, He led me out of all my debt over three years! It was like I woke up one day, and I was free!

God did it for me, and He will do it for you. Many of the principles that you need are in this book, but you will also need to study your Bible. The Word of God is the true blueprint for our lives. The Word shows us who we are and how to live. It shows us our shortcomings and areas where we must repent and change. The Scriptures help us to look more and more like God every day.

Hear the Word and Do It

When you pick up the Bible, it's like looking in the mirror. When you look in a mirror, you see your image. It's the same with the Bible. According to John 1:1, the WORD IS GOD. When you read the Word, you look at who you should be and how you should live. Your thoughts and ways should align with God's thoughts and His ways. That's when your life and finances will change for the better.

Often, Christians conform to the ways of this world and refuse to be transformed by the Word of faith. The Bible even speaks of people no longer listening to sound doctrine or good teaching. Instead, they follow their own desires and look for teachers who will tell them whatever they want to hear. They reject and turn away from the truth and turn to man-made fabrications and lies (2 Timothy 4:3-4).

If we hear the Word and choose not to do what it says, it's like looking in a mirror, seeing your face, then walking away and forgetting how you look. The Bible warns not just to hear or read the Word. Do what it says! Those who intently feed on the Word, which brings freedom, and do not become careless listeners who forget what it says, but abide in it, will be favored and blessed in what they do (James 1:22-25). In other words, a blessed person is a hearer *and* doer of the Word. And those who do what it says will always walk in blessings, prosperity, and freedom.

The world tries to paint a picture of what it looks like to be blessed, and it boils down to money and material possessions—a big house, a nice car, designer clothes, college degrees, or a successful career. However, pursuing material possessions can never lead to true happiness or satisfaction. True fulfillment can only be attained through a relationship and fellowship with God, achieved through His Son, Jesus Christ. Blessed are those who trust in the Lord and put their complete confidence in Him (Jeremiah 17:7). They hear the Word and do what it says (Luke 11:28). They will walk with wisdom and be prosperous and successful in what they do (Joshua 1:8).

Silence All Unbelief

Unbelief is the greatest hindrance to receiving debt freedom and living in God's true abundance. Unbelief hinders our prayers and the ability of God to work things out in our lives. So, as I became enlightened about God's will concerning money and debt, I had to silence all thoughts and voices of doubt, fear, and unbelief. I had to ignore the voices of people who didn't believe that living in this world without debt was possible. I can no longer follow the opinion of anybody if it doesn't align with the Scriptures. Every choice I make, particularly those related to finances, ought to be grounded in the teachings of the Word of God.

On your journey to debt freedom, you will be tested to see if you really believe you can owe no man anything but love. You will face challenges, uncertainties, and moments when you must prove you believe, without a doubt, that God will supply all your needs according to His riches in Christ Jesus. You may encounter Christians who don't know the truth about debt or those who know the Word but choose to go their own way, and they will try to convince you to do the same. But you must be strong in the Lord and stand on what you know and believe. You may encounter financial advisors who will try to steer you toward a worldly perspective on money and debt. But you must stand on the Word no matter what others think.

Remember: God will make a way! Be courageous, stand still, and know that He is God. Only believe, and you will see the glory of God! He has good plans for you, *"plans to prosper you and not to harm you, plans to give you hope and a future"* (Jeremiah 29:11). So don't get discouraged, for God is with you and will help you. He makes a way in the wilderness, in the desert, during the famine, during a recession, in the good and bad times. He will make a way out of no way!

Getting Out Won't Be Easy

When you try to get out of debt and live according to biblical financial principles, the world won't let you go easily. I recall when my husband embarked on his journey to get out of debt. He was focused and determined. He paid off over $40,000 in credit card debt and sold all the rental properties that had mortgages on them. He cut up all his credit cards and said goodbye to dependence on credit. All he had left to do was pay off our home mortgage. He had a plan. Every time he made extra money from his construction business, he put it to the side to pay off the mortgage. He was starting to send large amounts to the mortgage company that he directed toward the principal only. Obviously, the mortgage company could see that he was trying to pay it off. So, they sent him a "payment holiday." In other words, they sent him a letter stating he could skip a payment. We had never heard of a mortgage company voluntarily allowing you to skip a payment. But they didn't want him to pay it off. They were making too much money from the interest.

The world does not want us to come out of that system. It is too lucrative for those at the top, who lend all the money. The idea of the bank not wanting my husband to pay off the mortgage reminded me of Pharaoh and how he refused to let the Israelites go. He refused to let the Israelites go despite the plagues caused by divine intervention. Pharaoh was determined to hold on to his slaves—because if he let them go, it would affect the economy of Egypt. The Israelite slaves were an important source of cheap forced labor, contributing to the economic development and stability of the region.

The bank did not want to let my husband out easily. But they would not trick him with the "keep your money in your pocket" trick. He was almost out of debt. He knew too much and had come too far to turn back. The bank wanted him to continue to carry a balance because that's how they make money. But my husband began to pay even more money toward the principal. He was determined to get out of debt and "owe no man anything" so he could walk in the fullness of the blessing! Psalm 112:1-3 says, *"Blessed are those who fear the LORD, who find great delight in his commands. Their children will be mighty in the land; the generation of the upright will be blessed. Wealth and riches are in their houses, and their righteousness endures forever."*

For too many years, I thought that using other people's money was the path to wealth and riches. And yes, I made a lot of money using lines of credit, credit cards, and leveraging debt. But it didn't bring true wealth and riches. It brought fear into my life. I was always running and laboring after the next dollar. I was ruled by money, which brought misery because I never had enough. Unfortunately, I thought debt was the way of life and approved by God. But the Holy Spirit led me to the truth. True riches originate from God and are what heaven bestows or gives to us. When God blesses us, we are truly rich with no sorrow added to it.

Jesus draws a distinction between true riches and worldly wealth in Luke 16:11: *"So if you have not been trustworthy in handling worldly wealth, who will trust you with true riches?"* True riches are not measured by the size of your house, the kind of car you drive, or how much money you have in your bank account, but by how much you have deposited in your heavenly bank account. Jesus told us not to lay up treasures on earth for ourselves, where moths and rust can decay and thieves can break in and steal. But lay up treasures in heaven (Matthew 6:19-21).

We will someday give an account of how we have stewarded our resources on this earth and whether we have honored God and His Word. As I faced my staggering debt problem, it felt like God showed up and asked me to give an account of how I managed His money. Like the prodigal son in Luke 15:11-32, I was in a dilemma. I had no more money, didn't want to do hard labor, and was ashamed of my position. Like this wasteful son, it was time for me to return to my heavenly Father, repent, and be restored.

Have Faith in God

It would take mountain-moving faith to break the yoke of debt from my life. But Jesus tells us in Mark 11:22, *"Have faith in God."* What looked difficult for me was easy with God. He made the heavens and earth by His great power. There is nothing too difficult for God! He made a highway in the middle of the Red Sea. He raised the dead back to life. So, surely, He can get me out of debt and bless me so that I will never have to borrow again. *"With man this is impossible, but not with God; all things are possible with God"* (Mark 10:27).

Jesus said, if you have faith the size of a mustard seed, you can move mountains or whatever is in your way, and nothing will be impossible for you (Matthew 17:20). Faith to move mountains begins with believing that God hears your prayers. And whatever you ask for, believe it's already yours. Before you see it manifested, you must believe that you have it. Believing you have it before you see it is the essence of faith (Hebrews 11:1). Jesus exhorts us to have steadfast faith in the power and love of God. As true believers, we must be fully persuaded that God will keep His promises and show up for us in our time of need.

Before getting out of debt, I believed I could get out. I was still more than $100,000 in debt when I began to say out loud, "I am debt-free." I would speak to my bills and tell them to "Be gone." I didn't think my debt would simply disappear, nor was I trying to get out of paying my debts. Instead, I was demonstrating strong faith. I had unwavering confidence in God that He would lead me out of all my debt. Just like Jesus spoke to a fig tree, and it withered away with a word, I spoke and trusted that my mountain of debt was moving out of my way. I believe that my faith-filled words set things into motion, and the Lord started to arrange things supernaturally so that I could get out of debt. The Bible says we should call things that are not as though they were (see Romans 4:17). So, day after day, even though my debt was still visible, I said, "I am out of debt, and all my needs are met!"

My words were filled with faith — like the woman with an issue of blood whose faith-filled words set her healing in motion. She had dealt with her health issues for 12 long years and spent all her money trying to get well. She had done all she could do in her own strength. Then, she decided to try Jesus! She pushed through a crowd and said, *"If I only touch His garment, I can be healed."* It was her confidence in the power of God and her faith-filled words that initiated her divine healing. Her faith was so strong that it got the attention of Jesus. He turned to her and said, *"Your faith has made you whole"* (Matthew 9:20-22). I believe that this woman's encounter with Jesus brought wholeness to her life spiritually, physically, and financially. She put her faith in God, and it made all the difference.

Whatever He Tells You to Do, Do It

I noticed that when the patriarchs and leaders in the Bible needed God to move in their lives, God always gave them instructions that went against their natural or worldly wisdom. Most of the time, if God tells you to do something, it will sound crazy and seem impossible. Because whatever God tells you to do, you will need faith to do it. For example, in 1 Kings 17, the widow was in so much debt that the creditors were coming to enslave her sons. She went to the man of God to ask what to do because she trusted that he would hear from God. She told him that all she had of any value was a small jar of oil. Then, he tells her to gather as many pots as she can from her neighbors and fill them with the oil she has. That command didn't sound reasonable. But she did exactly what the man of God told her to do.

How do you fill pot after pot with such a small jar of oil? Without God, YOU CAN'T. However, by faith, YOU CAN! As long as she had empty pots, that oil kept flowing. When there were no more available pots, the oil stopped. It was a miracle!

And when it came to getting out of my debt, I needed a miracle, too! I was in so much debt. I didn't see how I could get out without working like a slave day in and out for many, many years to come. Like this woman, I needed an answer to my problem to be downloaded from God. The prophet gave her a solution, and she did what he told her. As a result of her obedience, she got out of debt. I learned from this widow: Whatever God tells you to do, do it!

Then there is the Bible account of the transformation of water into wine at the wedding at Cana (John 2:1-11). It was the first miracle attributed to Jesus. When the wine was gone at the wedding, Jesus' mother said to Him, *"They have no more wine."* Then she told the servants, *"Whatever He says to you, do it."* Jesus said to the servants, *"Fill the jars with water."* So they filled them to the brim. Then he told them, *"Now draw some out and take it to the master of the banquet."* They did so, and the master of the banquet tasted the water that had been turned into wine.

How does water turn into wine? What Jesus told them to do didn't make any sense, but it "made faith." In other words, it didn't make sense naturally, but when they obeyed, the supernatural happened.

I gleaned another great lesson from the Bible story about Naaman in 2 Kings 5. He was commander of the army of the king of Aram. His king considered him a great man, honorable, and highly respected. He was also a man of courage, but he worshiped other gods and had leprosy. Naaman wanted to be healed. So, he went to see the prophet, Elisha. He stood at the prophet's door, waiting for him to come outside. But the prophet didn't even come out of his house. Instead, Elisha sent a message to Naaman telling him, *"Go and wash yourself seven times in the Jordan River. Then your skin will be restored, and you will be healed of your leprosy"* (2 Kings 5:10, NLT).

But Naaman became angry and walked away. You see, Naaman was a well-respected man of valor. So, I'm sure he didn't expect what seemed like a cold welcome from the prophet. First, the prophet didn't greet him at the door. And second, he wasn't expecting to be told to get into the dirty Jordan River to wash. So, he turned and walked away in a rage.

The command Naaman was given was simple and easy to do, but he was prideful. All he had to do was obey and dip seven times in the Jordan River, and he would have been healed. Naaman's officers tried to reason with him and said, *"Sir, if the prophet had told you to do something very difficult, wouldn't you have done it? So, you should certainly obey him when he says simply, 'Go and wash and be cured!' So Naaman had a change of heart and went down to the Jordan River and dipped himself seven times, as the man of God instructed him"* (vv. 13-14, NLT). And he was healed!

I learned from Naaman that to obey God, I must put my pride aside. When you need the favor of God, the way to get it is to humble yourself before the Lord. His response to our prayer requests may be surprising and go against our limited wisdom and understanding. Often, His answer causes deep soul-wrestling and exposes our pride, doubts, and fears. In fact, His answer may not even seem like an answer. We may expect His answers to look different. But the Lord's unexpected answers always align with His Word and bring joy. Jesus promised, *"Ask, and you will receive, and your joy will be complete"* (John 16:24b). Sometimes, the path to receiving what you want may seem hard and painful, but in the end, there is joy.

My Way Out of Debt

I will never forget it. It was a summer day in 2010. I had taken my three children to see an animated movie (a kid's movie) at a theater near my home. I was sitting there with them, not paying attention to the screen because I had other things on my mind, like my debt. But as I was sitting there, I began to hear the Lord speak to my Spirit. I was sensitive to His voice during this time because I waited patiently for an answer to my financial situation. Then, suddenly, I heard God's voice clearly say, "File for bankruptcy." I know God's voice, and I heard it loud and clear!

You may be saying, "He told you what?!" Many Christians would find this hard to believe because bankruptcy is considered taboo or unacceptable for believers. I felt this way, too. I felt this way because some people file for bankruptcy to avoid paying their debts. I even thought about what happens to the creditor who doesn't get their money back if someone files for bankruptcy, especially Chapter 7 bankruptcy. I felt that if I borrowed the money, I was responsible for paying it back somehow. The thought of filing for bankruptcy never crossed my mind. So, I couldn't wait to get out of that theater to pray about what I had just heard. I had many questions for God, and believe me, He answered every one of them.

I was initially hesitant to share that I filed for bankruptcy due to the social stigma associated with it, especially among believers. However, as I delved into the Bible, I discovered that debt cancellation and forgiveness are recurring themes in both the Old and New Testaments. God's heart is for the release of debts and the relief of those in need. Even though bankruptcy is common in the United States, it is often seen as shameful. People who file for bankruptcy are often seen as irresponsible, immoral, dishonest, and lazy. I felt the same way in the past—that it was a matter of integrity for people to pay their debts. But my mind was about to change.

I thought, "There has to be another way to get out of debt." However, I remembered from examples in the

Scriptures that whatever God tells you to do, you should do it. But I prayed that God would give me understanding and proof from the Word that filing bankruptcy was the right path. In my search, I found that the word "bankruptcy" is nowhere in the Bible. However, I discovered that debt cancellation and debt forgiveness are central themes in both the New and Old Testaments.

In the Old Testament, God directed the Israelites to observe a "Year of Release" every seventh year, during which debts were canceled and people were set free from financial burdens. This practice highlighted God's desire to prevent long-term indebtedness and provide a fresh start for those in hardship. *"At the end of every seven years you must cancel debts. This is how it is to be done: Every creditor shall cancel any loan they have made to a fellow Israelite. They shall not require payment from anyone among their own people because the* LORD*'s time for canceling debts has been proclaimed. You may require payment from a foreigner, but you must cancel any debt your fellow Israelite owes you"* (Deuteronomy 15:1-3).

This command for a release from debt came directly from God and was not established or dictated by creditors or man-made laws—this was simply *God's release!* It is clear from Deuteronomy 15 that God is pleased when His people are released from their debts! God had a plan to keep His children from becoming hopelessly in debt. He provided relief for the poor so they wouldn't be hopelessly poor forever. No one was to be in debt for more than seven years. However, many people today are in so much debt that they will never recover in this lifetime—without God.

God expected His people to lend freely, but at the end of every seven years, they were required to forgive every debt and require no repayment. If they lent money to a stranger or foreigner, they could expect payment even during the Lord's

Year of Release. However, the children of Israel were released from the continuous bondage of poverty and the oppression of unmanageable debts. God desired that no one among His people remained poor. He intended for those with financial means in the community to relieve those in need. God promised to bless those with wealth if they kept His commands; they would always be able to lend and never have to borrow. He promised they would rule over many nations, but none would rule over them (Deuteronomy 15:3-4).

In addition to the Lord's Year of Release every seven years, God also declared a Year of Jubilee, which occurred after seven cycles of seven years. Jubilee meant freedom, release, and restoration. In the Year of Jubilee, all debts were forgiven, slaves were freed, and property was returned to its original owners (Leviticus 25:1-13). The Year of Jubilee was another reminder that God does not want people perpetually enslaved to one another. The Lord said several times in Leviticus 25, *"You shall not oppress one another."* He desires that we love and help each other without seeking personal gain.

God expects wealthy people to generously lend to their poor brethren in a manner that is sufficient to meet their needs. God told the children of Israel: *"Give generously to them and do so without a grudging heart; then because of this the* Lord *your God will bless you in all your work and in everything you put your hand to"* (Deuteronomy 15:10). God promised that those who lend and give cheerfully to the needy in their land would be blessed and would always be able to lend and never have to borrow! A person who only lays up treasure for himself is not rich toward God (see Luke 12:21).

Bankruptcy Is a Release

The similarities between the Lord's Year of Release, the Year of Jubilee, and Chapter 7 bankruptcy are plain to see.

Each is a *release* from unpaid debts. With bankruptcy, debtors are released from debt obligations and personal liability when they receive a bankruptcy discharge. This debt discharge is a permanent order, and creditors cannot contact the debtor or take any further action to collect the debts, or they could be subject to punishment for contempt. Similarly, in the Bible, all lenders *released* their debtors from their debt obligations every seven years.

It was much easier to obtain a release from debts in the Old Testament than filing for Chapter 7 bankruptcy today. Bankruptcy law has changed many times and now allows for the discharge of certain debt obligations, but not all of them (tax debt, student loan debt, and domestic support debt are excluded). In some cases, possessions must be sold to cover the debt. However, in the Bible days, there were no court proceedings to attend, no need for lawyers, no judges, no filing fees, and no requirement for assets to be sold to repay creditors. The debt was canceled entirely, period. It is apparent that Chapter 7 bankruptcy laws were initially based on biblical principles.

Some Christians argue that Christians should not file for bankruptcy. They often misinterpret or misuse Psalm 37 as proof that bankruptcy violates biblical principles, which is not the intended message of the Psalm. However, this Psalm does address borrowing and lending. Psalm 37:21 says, *"The wicked borrow and do not repay, but the righteous give generously."* This verse compares the wicked with the righteous. It reveals that a wicked person borrows AND either can't repay or won't, suggesting dishonesty and irresponsibility. On the other hand, the righteous are lenders, generous, and givers: *"They are always generous and lend freely; their children will be a blessing"* (v. 26).

What's wicked is to go into debt because of greed and not being content with what you have. If you read the Psalm in its entirety, you will see that it's wicked not to trust the Lord and wait on Him to give you the desires of your heart. Wicked people beg and borrow for what they want and need but ultimately come to ruin. However, the righteous spend their days resting under the Lord's care, and even during famine and economic downturns, they prosper.

God cannot be against forgiving a loan, or He would not have commanded the Israelites to cancel debts every seven years. If God were against the forgiveness of debts, He would not have established the Year of Jubilee, which came every 50th year, fully releasing every borrower from their debts, releasing all slaves, and returning property to those who owned it (Leviticus 25:1-13).

The Year of Jubilee was also a year of rest—to honor the Lord. Everyone got to rest during this year and could start the following year with a clean slate. During this Sabbath year, the Israelites were prohibited from planting in the fields or trimming their vineyards. Even the land had a year of rest. They were to eat whatever the land produced during the year of rest.

God promised if they obeyed and allowed the land to rest, the land would give good crops, and they could eat as much as they wanted during the time of rest. God assured them saying, *"I will send you such a blessing in the sixth year that the land will yield enough for three years. While you plant during the eighth year, you will eat from the old crop and will continue to eat from it until the harvest of the ninth year comes in."* (Leviticus 25:21-22). Look at God! He promised them a great blessing— a crop that would be sufficient for three years. They didn't have to work, plow, plant, or harvest for years because Jehovah Jireh would provide.

God takes rest seriously. He doesn't want us to get caught up in thinking we can provide for ourselves and trust in our own provision. God is God alone. He knows all about us, understands what we need, and always provides for those who trust Him. Even when the future seems uncertain, we must look to Him for help because He cares for us.

The Israelites went into captivity because they didn't observe these resting years (Leviticus 26). They reaped the consequences because they didn't trust that God would provide. Today, people go into deep debt and suffer because they don't seek the Lord for everything they need. We don't rest in the provision that He has made but try to find our own way and make our own rules to follow.

Debt is not a money problem; it's a contentment problem. When you don't find true satisfaction in God, you will run after stuff paid for with debt to satisfy your longings and make you content. But spending money in the pursuit of happiness will never fill your heart's desires. We were created to worship and long for God only. Understand me. There's nothing wrong with having things as long as things don't have you. Spending with borrowed money doesn't bring lasting happiness but brings stress and anxiety.

Debt Forgiveness Is God's Idea

There is no mountain of debt so large that God's grace can't tear it down. There is no financial pit so deep that God's grace can't pull you out. You don't have to feel overwhelmed or be paralyzed with fear. There is hope. You can get out of debt and stay out. God wants to give you a new beginning just like He did for me. And trust me, you can overcome the shame. If you repent and turn to God with a surrendered heart, God's grace will see you through.

God gave me a revelation about debt forgiveness and freedom through the finished work of Jesus Christ. He revealed to me that Jesus is our Jubilee! On the Day of Atonement, Jesus entered the Holy of Holies in the very presence of God by His own blood and obtained eternal redemption for us all. So, we have been redeemed from the curse of sickness, death, poverty, and all debt!

In Leviticus 25, the Year of Jubilee occurred every 50th year on the Day of Atonement. On this day, the Lord commanded Israel to blow the trumpet of the Jubilee, proclaiming deliverance from bondage and that *all debts were canceled*. Today, Jesus is our Jubilee! He has set us free from all sins and debts! Colossians 2:13-15 explains it beautifully: *"When you were dead in your sins and in the uncircumcision of your flesh, God made you alive with Christ. He forgave us all our sins, having canceled the charge of our legal indebtedness, which stood against us and condemned us; he has taken it away, nailing it to the cross. And having disarmed the powers and authorities, he made a public spectacle of them, triumphing over them by the cross."*

Yes! God forgives sins and debts! He cancels every one of them and allows you to go free of charge! Jesus already paid the price. So you don't have to pay. There is nothing the powers and authorities can do about it. Jesus has triumphed over them through the cross. *"So if the Son sets you free, you will be free indeed"* (John 8:36). Just like in the Year of Jubilee, you are *released* from sin, debt, and its consequences in your life; you are *restored* into full fellowship with God; you are *released* from all bondage of the enemy; and you have access to the *full provision* of God. You don't have to struggle under the weight of debt and loans. The trumpet has been sounded! You have been liberated! You have been released from the need to carry heavy burdens.

When I cried out to God in despair and repented because of my overwhelming debt, God forgave me and gave me a way out. I didn't have to pay it back. I couldn't pay it—the debt was too big. This is the picture of what Jesus did for us all on the cross. We were sinners and rebellious towards God, and the wages (the cost) of sin was death. We couldn't pay the price it took to get us out of the debt we owed God. Silver or gold was not enough. Only the blood of Jesus could cover the ransom needed to save our lives. Jesus paid it all! Jesus came to pay a debt He did not owe because we owed a debt we could not pay.

Jesus gives us a parable in Matthew 18 about the extent to which we should forgive one another. When Peter famously asked Jesus how many times he should forgive a brother or sister who has sinned against him, he suggested, "Up to seven times?" Jesus answered, "Not seven times, but seventy times seven." This is a sharp warning to those who might think forgiveness is possible on limited terms. There is no limit! In this parable, Jesus teaches some very important principles of the kingdom of heaven that we must apply today.

"Therefore, the kingdom of heaven is like a king who wanted to settle accounts with his servants. As he began the settlement, a man who owed him ten thousand bags of gold was brought to him. Since he was not able to pay, the master ordered that he and his wife and his children and all that he had be sold to repay the debt.

At this the servant fell on his knees before him. 'Be patient with me,' he begged, 'and I will pay back everything.' The servant's master took pity on him, canceled the debt and let him go" (Matthew 18:23-27).

As you can see, in the kingdom of God, debts are CANCELED! The king forgives the enormous debt. In a marvelous act of mercy, the king wipes the debt off the books and gives a jubilee to this servant who is about to be sold along with his family to repay the debt. The servant offered to pay it all back, but his master felt compassion for him and chose to pardon and let him go free! That's the kind of God we serve! His ways are not our ways, and His thoughts are not like ours.

Jesus continued the parable:

"But when the man left the king, he went to a fellow servant who owed him a few thousand dollars. He grabbed him by the throat and demanded instant payment. His fellow servant fell before him and begged for a little more time…. But his creditor wouldn't wait. He had the man arrested and put in prison until the debt could be paid in full. When some of the other servants saw this, they were upset. They went to the king and told him everything that had happened. Then the king called in the man he had forgiven and said, 'You evil servant! I forgave you that tremendous debt because you pleaded with me. Shouldn't you have mercy on your fellow servant, just as I had mercy on you?' Then the angry king sent the man to prison to be tortured until he had paid his entire debt" **(Matthew 18:28-34, NLT).**

At the end of this parable, Jesus warns, *"This is how my heavenly Father will treat each of you unless you forgive your brother or sister from your heart"* (Matthew 18:35). We must take the warning in this parable seriously and not skip over it like it's a good Bible story. God has extended His grace and forgiven us of our sins against Him. So, we are to extend that same grace and forgiveness to one another. James 2:13 warns us that judgment will be merciless to one who has shown no mercy. The truth is that God forgives us of the most enormous debt imaginable—all our sins—whether murder, lying, stealing, sexual immorality, adultery, fornication, pornography, and much more. He forgives us whether the offense was our willful actions or innocent mistakes. If God is generous with His forgiveness of us, then surely we can extend that same forgiveness to each other. And if God forgives sins, surely He forgives the $20,000, $100,000, or even millions of dollars of debt we owe!

If it were up to us, we would not forgive but would hold grudges and keep people bound by the mistakes they make. Mankind finds it hard to pardon those who have offended them. But not God. We can rebel against Him, but He allows us to repent and return to Him. We forgive and cannot forget. But God graciously forgives, pardons us from our sins, and remembers it no more. The Lord himself says, *"For my thoughts are not your thoughts, neither are your ways my ways"* (Isaiah 55:8, KJV). God's ways and His thoughts are higher. Even though man is made in God's image, the ways and nature of God transcend that of man. It can be difficult for us to understand the acts of God and how He would allow man to go free from debts.

Those who can pay off their debts *should* pay them! But those who can't—those who are struggling in a pit of debt, feeling lost and ashamed—can cry out to a compassionate and merciful God and receive help in their time of need. God can give you supernatural debt cancellation if you only believe! If you put your trust in people or the world's system to get you out, they will let you down. Have faith in God. He has unlimited ways to bring you out of debt, and there is nothing man can do about it.

One thing I know for sure: God wanted me out of debt and helped me get out! I went from having ten maxed-out credit cards, feeling anxious and fearful, being under intense pressure, and wondering if there was any hope, to becoming debt-free in three years! Finally, I had no more debt bills coming in the mail. My emotional and financial crisis was over! I no longer lived from day to day, worried about the next paycheck to pay back creditors. The days of waking up every morning thinking about money and bills were over. My days of toil, worry, and having a survival mentality were behind me. I was free and could finally rest!

Chapter 6

The Freedom to Rest

THE PARTING OF THE RED SEA IS ONE OF THE MOST spectacular miracles in the Bible! It was one of many miraculous demonstrations of God's power and determination to liberate His people. It showed that God is willing to intervene in extraordinary ways to ensure the freedom and well-being of His chosen ones.

God delivered the Israelites out of slavery to a new life free from bondage. But He didn't get them out of Egypt to be broke, beggars, or borrowers. He didn't bring them out of slavery to a life of poverty and deprivation. God directed them to ask their Egyptian neighbors for silver, gold, and clothing. The Lord gave the people such favor in the sight of the Egyptians that they granted their request. So, they came out of Egypt *loaded* with great riches—with jewels of gold and of silver from the Egyptians at the command of the Lord.

The story of the Exodus serves as a testament to God's faithfulness, His power to deliver His people from oppression, and His desire for them to live in freedom and prosperity in every way. God heard their cry and delivered them from their enemies. Psalm 105:37 (NKJV) says, *"He brought them out with silver and gold, and there was none feeble among His tribes."* They plundered the Egyptians of all their wealth. And after 430 years of oppressive slavery, they left Egypt whole!

Let My People Go

In Egypt, the people of God were in an impossible situation. They were trapped in slavery with no place to turn. But God sent Moses to tell Pharaoh to *"Let my people go."* Pharaoh said, "No," time and time again. But no one can stand against God. No one! And with His incredible power and might, God rescued and delivered His people. That's what God did for me too!

I didn't mention this before. But before I filed for Chapter 7 bankruptcy, I met with a bankruptcy attorney. After discussing my case with her, she said I didn't qualify to file because my debt was consumer debt. She left the room to discuss the case with other colleagues. As soon as she stepped out, I prayed to God. I said, "Lord, you told me to do this. So, you'll have to make a way out of no way. You are my lawyer, and I need your help!" After what felt like an hour, the lawyer stepped back into the room, saying, "We can file the case!"

That wasn't the only obstacle I would face. After I filed for bankruptcy, I appeared twice in court in front of a judge alongside my lawyer. The first time I appeared, the judge said, "No." The judge explained that my case for Chapter 7 bankruptcy was denied because my debt was consumer debt. I didn't have any property the court could sell or liquidate. But I knew the Lord had directed me to file. So, I left the courtroom that day, knowing that man's NO was not God's

NO. I prayed on my way home, cast my cares to God, and didn't give up hope. Months later, I received a letter from the court stating that I had been granted a discharge. I could finally GO FREE!

I was out of debt! God set me free. I followed the instructions of the Holy Spirit, and now I am free! I no longer have debt chains holding me. I can go to sleep and wake up without creditors on my mind. My anxiety is gone. I no longer stay up at night wondering how I will repay creditors. There is no more fear. I closed every one of those credit accounts. Creditors can no longer call me, asking for what I owe them. No more debt bills are coming in the mailbox. I pay cash for everything. I went from depending on other people's money to trusting God to supply all my needs. I am finally at peace. *"If my people, who are called by my name, will humble themselves and pray and seek my face and turn from their wicked ways, then I will hear from heaven, and I will forgive their sin and will heal their land"* (2 Chronicles 7:14). I can finally rest.

Now, I allow the Holy Spirit to teach me how to handle finances God's way. I approach my financial decisions with a renewed mind that no longer conforms to the ways of this world. My mindset has shifted to focus on how God says I should navigate my finances. I discovered the kingdom's way of managing money and possessions. I am no longer brainwashed to believe that using debt is the only way to live in this world. I found Scriptures in the Bible that point to a better way—a way that glorifies God, paves the way to a more secure future, and helps me live a fuller, more joyful life!

God wants us out of debt so He can be God alone. He is a faithful God and a good Father who cares for His children. One of Satan's strategies is to get our eyes off God as a provider, causing us to focus on our financial needs and problems. Instead of looking to God as the supplier of our needs, Satan wants our thoughts consumed by lack and limited resources. Satan will attack our finances to take our eyes off God and make us fear that He won't come through. Worry and fear keep us running to the world to meet our needs. But God promises never to leave us or forsake us. He promises to supply all our needs according to His riches!

God doesn't need the help of banks, creditors, or payday loans to care for His children. He owns it all. God owns the whole world. He owns the cattle upon a thousand hills (Haggai 50:10). There is no lack in God's storehouse. His resources are unlimited. And He wants us to trust Him for our daily needs.

In the book of Exodus, God showed His devotion to the children of Israel as a covenant-keeping God. He called them His people and told Moses that He was coming to deliver them out of Egyptian captivity. He instructed Moses to tell Pharaoh, *"Let my people go."* God made it known that Israel belonged to Him and should be *free!* God was liberating His people from the harsh and demeaning yoke of Pharaoh so they could yoke up with Him. God set the Israelites free from a life where they depended on man for everything. The life lived by faith is a much lighter yoke and a much easier burden to carry than the heavy and burdensome yoke of self-centeredness, self-help, and independence from God.

When God liberated the people from bondage, He gave them instructions on how to live a godly life. God freed them from spiritual and physical servitude so they could serve the one true God. They were taught to be compassionate with foreigners, *"for you were slaves in the land of Egypt"* (Exodus 22:21). To remember slavery was to give them a moral sensitivity rather than a mark of shame. They were not to forget God but to remember *"for it is he who gives you the ability to produce wealth"* (Deuteronomy 8:18a).

When God supernaturally delivered them out of slavery, they left with the riches of Egypt. And God promised that if they were obedient to Him, He would bless and prosper them, their children, their crops, their livestock, and everything they possessed. God made a covenant to be with them, protect them, and prosper them in all they did.

God was leading the Israelites to a place of rest. But sadly, they griped and complained the whole time. God described them as a stubborn, nay-saying, and obstinate people. Even as they traveled in the wilderness for 40 years, headed toward the Promised Land, God never left their side and they lacked nothing. God's provisions included all the necessary sustenance, including food and water. The Lord told the children of Israel, *"During the forty years that I led you through the wilderness, your clothes did not wear out, nor did the sandals on your feet. You ate no bread and drank no wine or other fermented drink. I did this so that you might know that I am the Lord your God"* (Deuteronomy 29:5).

God wants us to know, trust, and believe that He is our Lord. He desires that we seek Him, reach out for Him, and find Him. He is never far away from any of us: *"For in him we live and move and have our being"* (Acts 17:28a). God showed the Israelites through many signs and wonders that they could depend on Him, and we can too. He is the same God today as He was yesterday.

The fact that the Israelites survived the plagues God sent on the Egyptians should have proved to them they could rely totally on God. He brought them safely through the Red Sea but slaughtered their enemies, the Egyptians. God showed them that they were favored, and He controlled their destiny. But even with the miraculous parting of the sea, the Israelites were afraid and murmured against their leader, Moses. The people said, *"If only we had died by the* LORD's *hand in Egypt! There we sat around pots of meat and ate all the food we wanted, but you have brought us out into this desert to starve this entire assembly to death"* (Exodus 16:3).

They had seen amazing miracles and escaped a horrible slave life, but all they could think about was meat and food! Almost as soon as the complaint came out of their mouths, the Lord graciously came to their aid again and provided them with manna—not just for that day but for the entire 40 years in the desert! God had led them into a place where they would have to depend wholly on Him for their daily needs. And once more, the Lord did not abandon them but proved to be a trustworthy provider.

God was trying to lead them to a place of rest—to know and trust that they could trust Him alone for everything! God was leading them out of slave life, where they had to sweat and toil for what they needed, into a rest that only He could provide. God's rest would bring complete wholeness to their lives. They would no longer have to labor for what they needed. God was leading them to the Promised Land— a land flowing with milk and honey, the land of more than enough! He was guiding them from a place of fear to freedom, provision, and rest!

God described the Promised Land as "good" and "spacious." It was a rich and fertile land where God's people would flourish and thrive economically. In this land, they would experience *no poverty* and *no lack;* It was filled with God's abundance of everything. They would experience a new way of life where they would no longer depend on man's natural limitations. God was bringing them to a place where they would find good things that they didn't have to struggle to get or borrow to receive! God was *giving* them the land:

"When the LORD your God brings you into the land he swore to your fathers, to Abraham, Isaac and Jacob, to give you— a land with large, flourishing cities you did not build, houses filled with all kinds of good things you did not provide, wells you did not dig, and vineyards and olive groves you did not plant—then when you eat and are satisfied, be careful that you do not forget the LORD, who brought you out of Egypt, out of the land of slavery" **(Deuteronomy 6:10-12).**

Imagine that! God promised them cities they didn't have to lift a finger to build, wells they didn't have to dig, vineyards they didn't plant, and houses—houses that were already fully furnished! God was *giving* them this good land to possess, not because they deserved it or were so good. *"It is not because of your righteousness or the uprightness of your heart that you go in to possess their land, but because of the wickedness of these nations that the LORD your God drives them out from before you, and that He may fulfill the word which the LORD swore to your fathers, to Abraham, Isaac, and Jacob"* (Deuteronomy 9:5, NKJV).

God planned to *give* them this land because He promised to give Abraham's descendants the land of Canaan. So, God told the children of Israel to "go in and possess the land." Just take over everything. It's already yours. Of course, there would be enemies in the land who needed to be defeated, but God told them to be strong and courageous. They wouldn't have to fight alone—the great and awesome God was with them. He promised, *"My Presence will go with you, and I will give you rest"* (Exodus 33:14).

God told them not to be afraid of the people in the land but to remember what God did to Pharaoh and all of Egypt. They had seen with their own eyes how the LORD brought them out with great signs and wonders and a mighty hand. He would do the same to all the people in the land of Canaan. The Lord promised, *"No one will be able to stand up against you; you will destroy them"* (Deuteronomy 7:24b).

I learned from the account of the Israelites escaping slavery that God wants His people free—free from debt. God can get us out supernaturally, with signs and wonders. Just like He allowed the Israelites to destroy the inhabitants of the Promised Land, He wants you to do the same with debt—destroy it. When you owe people money, they can stand against you, harm you, and cause you to be afraid. You will never be able to relax, quiet your mind, or rest until you get out of debt!

From Slavery to Freedom

The Israelites' journey from slavery to freedom was filled with trials and tribulations, but they needed to trust the process because they were not alone. God was leading them. In the wilderness, He led them with a cloud by day and fire by night. Their journey was filled with adversity, but they would become stronger and more mature because of their experiences.

When I was on my way out of debt slavery, it was not easy. I endured some ups and downs. But I learned humility and to trust God completely. It was a battle, but the battle was not mine alone. Just like Moses told the Israelites as they stood at the edge of the Red Sea, *"Stand firm and you will see the deliverance the LORD will bring you today.... The LORD will fight for you; you need only to be still"* (Exodus 14:13b-14).

Our job is to trust God and trust the process. God doesn't allow us to see the whole plan because He knows it would overwhelm us. When Pharaoh let the people go, God did not lead the people into the Promised Land using the nearest path, for God said, *"The people may have a change of heart when they see war and want to return to Egypt"* (Exodus 13:17, paraphrased). He knew the people would be fearful and want to turn back to captivity. So, God led the people through the wilderness instead.

After 400 years of bondage and deliverance from Egypt, the Lord led His chosen people to the edge of the Promised Land. They had God on their side, and it was finally time for them to inherit the land flowing with milk and honey that God promised to their forefathers. God's people would finally enter their rest.

But before the children of Israel could enter, they sent 12 spies to check out the land. Ten of the spies returned with a negative report and were afraid because they saw giants there. They whined because the people in the land were of great stature, and they felt like grasshoppers compared to them. They felt small and helpless. So, they influenced the rest of the congregation saying, *"We can't go up against them! They are stronger than we are!"* (Numbers 13:31, NLT) Then the congregation murmured and cried and were afraid to possess the land. Only two spies, Joshua and Caleb, believed they could defeat the people of the land with God's help.

God became angry because of their lack of faith and unbelief, and He swore they would never enter His rest. God was grieved by that generation and said, *"Their hearts are always going astray, and they have not known my ways"* (Hebrews 3:10). They failed to believe and trust in God's power and promises. They put more trust in what they saw in people than in the Lord who said, *"Go and possess the land!"* They refused to listen and obey. God was taking them to a place of blessings where they would experience *no lack.* But because of their *lack of faith,* no one from that generation was allowed to enter the Promised Land, except for Joshua and Caleb.

Let us learn from the mistakes of those who lacked the faith to rest in God's abundance. Just as God provided a land filled with blessings for the Israelites, He continues to offer us a life free from financial stress and anxiety. God is trying to *give us* the good life, which includes everything we need — just like He was trying to give them the good land.

The Israelites didn't have to make sure their credit report was good. Nor were they required to obtain a specific credit score. They didn't need to make an appointment with a banker or ask any man to borrow money to purchase the Promised Land. They didn't need help from any outside sources. God said to them, *"I have set the land before you. Go in and possess it."* They didn't need a loan to get this land. They would acquire this land with God's guidance and miraculous intervention.

The Key to God's Rest

The promised rest was assured to His people in the land of God — a place where their needs would be met abundantly. There would be no lack, and borrowing from others would be unnecessary as the Lord would bless them in their inheritance if they listened to and obeyed His voice (Deuteronomy 15:4-5). Having God's continual presence and being obedient to His voice was the key to rest. However, God's people lacked faith, hardened their hearts, and rebelled against God's voice. Consequently, they were denied entry into the Promised Land and missed their inheritance (Hebrews 3:11).

The Lord tried to show the Israelites what rest looked like when He established the Sabbath day. The Sabbath originated during the creation. God created the heavens and earth in six days; then He rested. He didn't rest because He was tired. He rested because all His work of creation was finished. He ceased from His labors. God established this principle of rest for His people. They were commanded to remember the Sabbath day and keep it holy. For six days, they would work, but on one day out of seven, they were to rest from their labors.

In the wilderness, God promised to rain food from the sky. He did this so they would trust Him for provision. Every day, they were to gather enough food for one day. The people gathered as much food as they needed every morning, and then the food melted away and was gone. But on the sixth day, they would gather and cook enough for two days so they could rest on the seventh day, the Sabbath.

Some people went out on the Sabbath to look for food anyway, but there was none. God had already provided a double portion. Then the Lord asked Moses (Exodus 16:28), *"How long will you refuse to keep my commands and my instructions?"* The Sabbath was made for man. They were to sit back, relax, and stay where they were. This day, they could stop all work, rest, spend time with family, and worship God. But man is always on a quest to find his own way to survive.

Hebrews 4 tells us that TODAY, there remains a rest for God's people. The Church today is being warned not to repeat the mistakes of the Israelites. We are urged to enter God's rest through faith (see Hebrews 4:1-11). TODAY, a promised rest is available to those of us who believe in Jesus as our Lord and Savior. But if we want to inherit the promises of God, we must first leave Egypt. We must stop trusting in ourselves or man for provision. The Bible tells us that the just shall live by faith. And without faith, it's impossible to please God. Unbelief hinders the power of God in our lives. In Mark 6:4-6, Jesus did not perform miracles due to the people's lack of faith.

Sadly, we can fail to enter God's "rest," too. The Israelites were our example. We are being warned TODAY not to walk in the same manner of unbelief as they did. They heard the good news that God was giving them the exceeding good land—a place where they would rest from their enemies. Their problem was they were fearful and did not mix faith with what they heard, so the message did not do any good (Hebrews 4:2). God was grieved with that generation because they had *"an evil heart of unbelief"* (3:12).

The Sabbath was a shadow of what was to come. The reality of the Sabbath rest is found in Christ (Colossians 2:17). Just as God sanctified the Sabbath day, He also sanctified Christ, and He became the sacrifice for our sins. Everyone who believes in Jesus Christ becomes the righteousness of God in Him (2 Corinthians 5:21). It is in Christ that we find rest from all our self-effort and laboring to please God. The Sabbath points to Jesus, who sets us free from sin, death, and this world system! Jesus came to free us from the curse of the law. He alone satisfies all the requirements of the law.

Jesus also came to rescue us from this earth-cursed system. As believers, we have been translated from the kingdom of darkness into the kingdom of His dear Son. We are children of God and kingdom citizens. We can now rest in Him not just one day but always because we have the promised Holy Spirit to lead us and guide us. We can rest if we listen to His voice and follow His commands. But if we don't, God vowed that, like the Israelites, we might never experience "His rest."

"Therefore, since the promise of entering his rest still stands, let us be careful that none of you be found to have fallen short of it.... Therefore, since it still remains for some to

enter that rest, and since those who formerly had the good news proclaimed to them did not go in because of their disobedience, God again set a certain day, calling it 'Today'.... 'Today, if you hear his voice, do not harden your hearts'" (Hebrews 4:1, 6-7).

God is telling us: TODAY, if you hear and don't harden your hearts, YOU can rest. So many voices are trying to lead us regarding money, wealth, prosperity, and all aspects of life. But Jesus says, *"My sheep listen to my voice; I know them, and they follow me"* (John 10:27) and *"a stranger will they not follow"* (v. 5, KJV). He speaks to you daily—if you will only listen. If you are a bona fide believer, you no longer need to struggle to meet your own needs. Believing in Jesus is the answer to all poverty and toil. Jesus promised that we can find rest in Him. He kindly invites us, gently calls us, and graciously compels souls to come to Him to find rest:

"Come to me, all you who are weary and burdened, and I will give you rest. Take my yoke upon you and learn from me, for I am gentle and humble in heart, and you will find rest for your souls. For my yoke is easy and my burden is light" (Matthew 11:28-30).

To believe in Christ is more than just walking to the altar on your day of salvation or declaring that you believe in Him. It is to surrender your life, humble yourself, and "come to" Him for everything you need. When Jesus left the earth, He didn't leave us alone. God sent the Holy Spirit to teach us and guide us so that we don't have to "do life" alone. The Holy Spirit is our advocate, our comforter, helper, teacher, and guide.

It is imperative to understand the work of the Holy Spirit as our helper. In Greek, the powerful word *paraclete* means one who comes alongside another. Jesus invites us to "yoke up" with Him. A yoke is a farming tool that joins two animals to share the workload evenly, which is better for strength and more excellent production. Taking the yoke of Jesus is like being side-by-side with Him, following where He guides through the Holy Spirit. When we are yoked to Him, we are led by Him. When we are led, we can be more effective and successful in what we are called to do.

The Holy Spirit guides us when we don't know which way to turn and gives us answers when we are lost. As we spend time in the Word, in prayer, and walking about, the Holy Spirit speaks to us and reveals God's will. His will is for us to live in freedom as His beloved children. As a child of God, you have rights to an inheritance. You can cry out to your Father in heaven and receive everything that was promised to you.

The Holy Spirit is the voice, the guide, who will lead you to everything that belongs to you! The Spirit would never lead you to become enslaved. Debt is slavery! You are God's daughter, His son, an heir, not a debtor. Galatians 4:6-7 says, *"Because you are his sons, God sent the Spirit of his Son into our hearts, the Spirit who calls out, 'Abba, Father.' So you are no longer a slave, but God's child; and since you are his child, God has made you also an heir."*

If you are saved, you have been adopted by God. You have a new identity. You are kin to Jesus! God raised you when He raised Christ from the dead. You are seated with God in heavenly realms in Christ Jesus (Ephesians 2:6). Jesus is seated at the right hand of God, and you are too!!! You are Christ's body and His co-heir. You're an heir with an inheritance. I will say again, "HEIRS DON'T NEED DEBT!" You don't have to beg the world for anything—you belong to the family of God!

You are no longer a slave! So, come out of debt! No matter what you need, you can cry, "Abba Father!" You have a Father in heaven who has an abundant supply of treasures and blessings waiting for you. All you must do is ASK for it: *"This is the confidence we have in approaching God: that if we ask anything according to his will, he hears us. And if we know that he hears us— whatever we ask—we know that we have what we asked of him"* (1 John 5:14-15).

If we fail to trust God and His promises fully, we become disobedient and forfeit our ability to enter His rest—just like the children of Israel who came out of the bondage of Egypt but could not enter the Promised Land. Like them, many Christians today trust in themselves and their self-effort and have failed to enter God's rest. The Bible says in Acts 7:51, *"You stiff-necked people! Your hearts and ears are still uncircumcised. You are just like your ancestors: You always resist the Holy Spirit."* Our ancestors boasted about being circumcised, but they had not circumcised their hearts to trust in God or their ears to hear and obey His voice.

The Holy Spirit was given to help us, guide us, enlighten us, persuade us, and lead us to the promises of God. Listening to the voice and following the teachings of the Holy Spirit are our keys to rest! So, the Bible warns us, *"do not harden your heart."* When the voice of God is ignored, resisted, and grieved, the sinner is left to reap the fruit of his doings.

Enter God's Rest

Don't miss God's rest. Get to know God through His Word and become aware of His voice so that you don't miss out because of unbelief. Hebrews 4:11 (KJV) says, *"Let us labor therefore to enter into that rest, lest any man fall after the same example of unbelief."* Your labor should be in prayer and in the Word of God, hearing it, and building your faith in God's promises. That's how you labor to enter God's rest.

We enter His rest by knowing, believing, and trusting in His promises and when we hear His voice, acting on it. Those who are not resting in God's promises, God will never enter His rest. This verse doesn't say to labor to build a house, pay bills, or struggle to get overtime pay. But it says, *"Let us labor to enter God's rest."*

This kind of faith demands that you rest from relying on your own works. You don't have to worry about what you will eat, drink, or wear; you must trust that God will provide. When you fear and don't trust God's provision, you will take matters into your own hands, which leads to borrowing and debt. But we must put our trust in someone who promised never to leave us or forsake us. *"Blessed is the one who trusts in the Lord"* (Jeremiah 17:7).

Your job is not your source. It is a channel through which blessings flow. Your bank account is not your security. Bank accounts rise and fall. The economy is good one day and bad the next. The stock market goes up and down based on confidence in the economy. None of this should matter to a believer; your confidence must be anchored in God. While everybody is scurrying around trying to figure out how to make it, you are depending solely on God as your never-ending supply. You are resting in the One who promised to supply all your needs according to His riches!

He Brought Them Out to Bring Them In

I learned a valuable lesson from the children of Israel. The first generation, under the leadership of Moses, received orders to "go," but failed to possess the Promised Land. They lacked the faith and faithfulness to receive what God was GIVING them. God brought them out of Egypt, the land of slavery, to get them to a place of freedom and peace: *"He brought us out from there to bring us in and give us the land he promised on oath to our ancestors"* (Deuteronomy 6:23). God wasn't just giving them land. He was bringing them into His complete care. God was leading them to a place where they would lack nothing. All they had to do was trust Him, and never again would they have to depend on anybody for anything. However, they wavered back and forth between belief and unbelief. They didn't have complete confidence in God's voice and instructions and missed their opportunity to rest in Him.

The next generation of Israelites, under the leadership of Joshua, entered the Promised Land—a place of liberty, protection, and abundance. God brought them from a dry place to a place of no lack. However, they returned to their old ways and mindsets and would not keep God's commands. He warned them that when they entered the good land they were not to go after other gods, the gods of the people around them (Deuteronomy 6:14). So, God instructed them to destroy the inhabitants of the land who didn't serve Him and to stomp out their corrupt culture. These inhabitants had rejected the true and living God and were being judged.

God wanted them to eradicate this people along with all their objects of worship. Why? Because He knew the impact their influence would have on the Israelites. The Israelites were a holy people, set apart to be the Lord's chosen possession, a special people above all people (Deuteronomy 7:6). But God knew that if they became neighbors with these people, mingling and making friends with these foreign nations, they would intermarry, make covenants with them, and would be turned away from following the true God to serve other gods of these Canaanite nations. Serving these other gods was forbidden behavior that came with consequences, including the wrath of God. It was clear that obedience would bring blessings, but disobedience would bring on the curse and chastisement.

God led the children of Israel to a land where they could rest and have everything they needed. But they began to conform to the ways of the world. Instead of relying on the only true God, they had more faith in the people around them. Before long, they had picked up the values and morals of the people inhabiting the land, which were not good.

They made treaties, agreements, and unions with the Canaanites and became ensnared and corrupted by money and idolatry (Exodus 34:12). Rather than serve the God who brought them out of Egypt, they served other gods. They made the God of heaven and earth so angry that He withheld His helping hand from them, which led to repeated defeats (Judges 2:1-3). And they were given over to slavery to serve their enemies, who plundered and robbed them. And they were bitterly distressed (Judges 2:12-15).

God had brought them out of Egypt with great signs and wonders to bring them to complete rest in His care, but they ended up stressed because they refused to trust and obey Him. Before he died, Joshua spoke a word from God to Israel. The Lord said to them (in my own words):

"I brought your people out of Egypt, the land of slavery, and brought you through the sea. You cried out because the Egyptians pursued you, but I destroyed them. You saw with your own eyes what I did to the Egyptians. Then, you remained in the wilderness for forty years. I protected you on your entire journey. I delivered you repeatedly from the hands

of your enemies. Then you crossed the Jordan River into Jericho and the Promised Land. I gave your enemies into your hands. You didn't have to fight with your own sword and bow. I drove them out before you—seven nations stronger than you. I gave you a land for which you did not toil, beg, or borrow, and cities you did not build, and you ate from vineyards and olive groves that you did not plant" **(Joshua 24:2-11, paraphrased).**

Then Joshua said to the people of God:
"Now fear the LORD and serve Him with all faithfulness. Throw away the gods your ancestors worshiped beyond the Euphrates River and in Egypt and serve the LORD. But if serving the LORD seems undesirable to you, choose for yourselves this day whom you will serve, whether the gods your ancestors served beyond the Euphrates or the gods of the Amorites, in whose land you are living. But as for me and my household, we will serve the LORD" **(Joshua 24:14-15).**

God is telling *us today:* "CHOOSE THIS DAY WHO YOU WILL SERVE!" Because you can't serve two masters. You can't serve God and money! If you seek and serve God, money or anything else you need won't be a struggle.

He Brought Me Out to Bring Me In

In 2010, I heard the voice of the Holy Spirit very clearly say, "You don't have any business being in debt." He led me to the truth in the Word about debt and finances. It was up to me to believe in God, be obedient, and not harden my heart. Even though nobody around me was debt-free, I believed what the Word of God said—that I could owe no man anything but love (Romans 13:8). Everybody I knew had a mortgage, credit card debt, car notes, and student loans. I didn't know anyone trying to get out of debt. But that didn't stop me. I held on to the TRUTH, and the truth set me free!

The story of the Israelites reminded me of my story. The same God that delivered them from Egyptian slavery delivered me out of $100,000 of credit card debt! My back was against the wall. I was facing the Red Sea and couldn't see any way out. My creditors were calling and coming after me. But I called on the name of the Lord, and He came down and rescued me. I studied the Word for three years and renewed my mind. The more I studied, the more I learned who I was in Christ.

I realized that heirs don't need debt! So, I refused to take another loan, regardless of my finances. I trusted that the God who fed 5,000 people with two fish and five loaves of bread could surely provide for me. The same Lord who led Peter to tax money in a fish's mouth will take care of my bills. I refused to reject God's Word that said, *"Keep out of debt and owe no man anything."* No matter what I need—whether a house, a car, clothes, or food—I am confident that God will make a way!

I didn't realize it, but during those three years of seeking Him and trusting Him, He led me to a place of rest. Jesus said, *"Come to me, all you who are weary and burdened, and I will give you rest.... Learn from me.... and you will find rest for your souls"* (Matthew 11:28-29). God brought me out of a bottomless pit so He could indeed be God in my life. He delivered me from the world system that supplied me with money and pleasures but no peace. God brought me out of debt-slavery and financial despair to bring me into His rest. *"He brought me up out of a horrible pit, out of the miry clay, and set my feet upon a rock, and established my steps"* (Psalm 40:2, KJV). He brought me out and placed my feet upon a firm foundation.

The Freedom to Rest

I had no rest until I got out of debt. It is exhilarating to no longer think about my creditors all day and night. I am so thankful to God for what He has done for me. If I had 10,000 tongues, I couldn't praise Him enough! I am free! I am free to trust Him! I am free to praise and worship Him! I am free to walk in my inheritance as a child of God. I am free to walk each day in His promises! I will never be broke, begging, borrowing, or lacking another day. I will always have what I need and more than enough! God is my Jehovah Jireh, my provider!

From now on, everything I receive, I will get by faith and God's favor! Faith is my new currency! *"Now faith is the substance of things hoped for, the evidence of things not seen"* (Hebrews 11:1, KJV). So, if I need a car, faith is the substance for it. If I need a house, I will get it by faith. Faith brings every vision to pass. If I need anything, I will do what Jesus did when He needed to feed thousands of people with only a few resources. I will take whatever I have, look to God, and expect Him to provide. I will not turn to debt. Instead, I will call on the Lord!

Jesus is inviting you to come out of debt, too! The same God who did it for me can give you rest, too! The key to rest is to discover the *right way* to live and the *right path* to follow and then get on that path and stay on it, and you will find rest for your soul (Jeremiah 6:16). The Word of God is the light for your path and Jesus is the way. He says, *"I am the way. I am the truth. I am the source of your life"* (John 14:6, paraphrased). Everything you seek and need is found in Him.

So, don't be like our ancestors, the Israelites. Don't throw away your confidence in Him. You will be richly rewarded if you persevere. And when you have done the will of God, you will receive what He has promised (Hebrews 10:35-36).

Jesus simply says, *"Come to me."* If you are weary and exhausted from working and doing it all alone: *"Come."* If you are weighed down with worry about how to meet your needs: *"Come!"* If you are worried about the future and whether you will have enough: *"Come!"* Jesus can remove your worries and your fears and give you peace. Take His yoke upon you, submit to Him, learn from Him, obey Him, and become like Him. He is the rest-giver!

You don't have to worry about how you will make it without debt. You have been given the secret to financial peace and rest: Obey the Word of God and follow the voice of the Holy Spirit! God is speaking to us every day through His Spirit. He gives us divine wisdom, directions, ideas, innovations, solutions, and witty inventions. He leads us to divine opportunities and guides us to riches stored in secret places. The Lord will show you His favor and give you His insight to get what you need when you need it.

God has an unlimited number of ways to take care of our needs. When Peter asked Jesus about paying taxes, Jesus told him what to do to cover their tax bills: *"Go to the sea, cast a hook, and take the first fish you catch. When you open its mouth, you will find a four-drachma coin. Take it and give it to them for My tax and yours"* (Matthew 17:27, BSB). Whatever you need, ASK GOD. And whatever He tells you to do, do it! Trust in God with all your heart, and rest easy!

Chapter 7

The Freedom to Enjoy Tea

GETTING OUT OF DEBT AND STAYING OUT IS ONE of the best decisions I have ever made. How does it feel to be out of debt? It's a relief! I no longer worry about creditors calling or receiving debt bills in the mail. My mind is entirely free from anxiety about making debt payments. I have no more pressure to go to work to make ends meet. I am relieved to know that nobody can hold anything over my head. I don't have to give a single thought to who I owe because I don't owe anybody anything. I have 100% freedom to make financial decisions without fear. Finally, I am free to yield to God and allow Him to guide me in spending, saving, and giving.

Before I got out of debt, I didn't have time to truly rest. I was too busy chasing ideas and goals that would bring satisfaction, contentment, accomplishment, and financial security. But now that I am debt-free, I spend more time pursuing the things of God. I took the time to survey my life, assess my priorities, and examine where my time, energy, and heart were going. I put aside all selfish ambition, put God first, and made Him the center of my life. All my passions, hopes, dreams, and desires rest in Him.

Now that I am debt-free, I have more time and energy to seek God, pray, and study the Bible. Chasing the Word, rather than chasing the world, has brought more satisfaction than I could have imagined. Every day, my soul hungers and thirsts for Him. The psalmist says in Psalm 63:1 (BSB), *"O God, You are my God. Earnestly I seek You; my soul thirsts for You. My body yearns for You in a dry and weary land without water."* And Jesus declared, *"I am the bread of life. He who comes to Me will never go hungry, and he who believes in Me will never be thirsty"* (John 6:35, NKJV).

My Desire for Tea

One day, soon after I got out of debt, I desired to sit with a cup of hot tea. However, I never drank hot tea before I got out of debt. But afterward, I would get up almost every morning and sit on my lounge chair by a window with a hot cup of tea while reading my Bible. Sitting down with a cup of hot tea represents peace and rest! With every sip of tea, I would bask in the goodness of God. I would think about how He got me out of so much debt and gave me a brand-new start. My heart overflowed with gratefulness for His grace and His mercy. His compassion and mercies are brand new every morning, and His lovingkindness and faithfulness renews day after day!

I believe that God gave me the desire for tea! The desire seemed to come out of nowhere. But this was just the beginning of God giving me the desires of my heart. Psalm 37:4 (ESV) holds a great promise: *"Delight yourself in the LORD, and he will give you the desires of your heart."* To delight myself in the Lord meant drawing closer to Him and finding peace, joy, satisfaction, and contentment in Him. It didn't mean getting everything I wanted. It meant aligning my will with His will and finding joy in His will being done.

In freedom, I had a radical shift in what I desired. Because I renewed my mind, turned from conforming to the world's ways, and determined to choose God's will, He transformed my desires to reflect His purpose for my life. God showed me what to desire! When we delight ourselves in the Lord, we are cleansed of selfish, prideful, and sinful desires. His desires become our desires, reflecting His goodness and grace.

Every sip of hot tea reminded me of the goodness of God! We see the evidence of His goodness demonstrated every day. We see it in the rising of the sun every morning. Whether times are good or bad—God is good! He is the same yesterday, today, and forever! His goodness doesn't change with the seasons! He is good all the time!

A righteous person may experience many troubles, but the Lord delivers them from them all. The righteous cry out to the Lord; He hears them and works things out for their good. In Psalm 34:8 David says, *"Taste and see that the LORD is good; blessed is the one who takes refuge in him."* David uses the metaphor of tasting to convey that just as one would taste food to know its flavor, one should seek a personal and direct experience of God's goodness.

The invitation to "taste and see" implies an experiential knowledge of God's goodness. It suggests that—like savoring a delicious meal or drink—we can experience and appreciate the goodness of the Lord by seeking Him, trusting in Him, and experiencing His faithfulness in our own lives. This verse encourages a personal and intimate relationship with God, where we are invited to actively engage with Him, seek His presence, and witness the goodness of the Lord. When you taste or see something, it isn't just something you've heard about—it's something you've *experienced for yourself.* It's a call to experience God's goodness firsthand through faith and trust in Him.

While enduring the challenges of deep credit card debt, I turned to the Lord. I earnestly cried out for deliverance from my financial struggles, and God graciously heard my plea. Like David, I sought the Lord, and He heard my cry and delivered me from all my fears (Psalm 34:4). Those who taste and see God's goodness have been through the fire; they have experienced life's ups and downs but have seen God make a way out of no way!

While it may seem unbelievable, I find gratitude in my experience of being in debt. This challenging journey has catalyzed the discovery of profound biblical principles and Scriptures that now serve as guiding lights in my life. And most of all, my experience is a testament to the redemptive power of faith in God. The Lord revealed a path to debt freedom, teaching me principles of stewardship, wise decision-making, and trust in His provision. Today, I live by these transformative lessons, which help me navigate my financial decisions with wisdom and reliance on God. I have indeed tasted and seen that the Lord is good, experiencing His goodness firsthand in the face of economic challenges.

I Shall Not Want

One day after I got out of debt, I was sitting by my window sipping a hot cup of tea, thinking about how God rescued my life from a pit of financial despair. I was so grateful for the freedom to sit with tea, no longer worried about meeting needs. And as I was meditating, God brought Psalm 23 (KJV) to my remembrance, and I began to ponder on it line-by-line:

"The LORD is my shepherd; I shall not want.
He maketh me to lie down in green pastures:
He leadeth me beside the still waters. He restoreth my soul:
He leadeth me in the paths of righteousness for His name's sake.
Yea, though I walk through the valley of the shadow of death,
I will fear no evil: for thou art with me; thy rod and thy staff
they comfort me.
Thou preparest a table before me in the presence of mine
enemies:
thou anointest my head with oil; my cup runneth over.
Surely goodness and mercy shall follow me all the days of
my life:
and I will dwell in the house of the LORD forever."

In the Bible, God compares His relationship with His people to sheep and a shepherd. We are called sheep because we are often misguided and follow anyone without thinking. It may be that sheep are incapable of providing their own needs. They need a shepherd to lead them to the pastures and beside the still waters. Sheep have no sense of direction and cannot defend themselves when danger arises. Sheep unwittingly tend to get lost, get in trouble, and wander away from the shepherd. Sheep need the shepherd to care for them when they are ill or injured and restore them when they have walked away from him. Isaiah 53:6 says, *"We all, like sheep, have gone astray, each of us has turned to our own way; and the LORD has laid on him the iniquity of us all."*

Like sheep, we can't make it without Jesus, the Good Shepherd. A good shepherd cares for his sheep so profoundly that he lays his life down for the sheep. Even if the sheep get off track and go their own way, the good shepherd mercifully leads them back into his care. First Peter 2:25 says, *"For you were like sheep going astray, but now you have returned to the*

Shepherd and Overseer of your souls." Like sheep, we need His direction, protection, and provision. When we allow the Lord to be our shepherd, we can confidently say, *"I shall not want."*

A good shepherd guides the sheep with his voice. The obedient sheep hear his voice, and no other voice will they follow (John 10:11, 14). If the sheep follow the voice of the Good Shepherd, the sheep will never want for anything. When we follow Him, we will tap into His ever-flowing, all-sufficient, unlimited heavenly provisions. Psalm 34:10 (KJV) says, *"The young lions do lack, and suffer hunger: but they that seek the LORD shall not want any good thing."* God-seekers will never have to worry about what we will drink, what we will eat, what we will wear, or where we will lay our head because we will have confidence that the Good Shepherd knows what we need and will provide.

My Cup Overflows

I recognized that even as I faced deep debt, in my darkest valley, the most challenging time in my life, God's presence was always there. He never left me. God is trustworthy. Even during difficult times, God will protect you and give you everything you need. David says in Psalm 23 that the Lord doesn't just give you what you need, He gives in abundance—until your cup overflows! A cup runs over when it cannot hold all that is being poured. God is generous with His love, grace, and provision. Ephesians 3:20 describes God as the One *"who is able to do immeasurably more than all we ask or imagine."* This overflow of blessings is not just limited to material possessions or temporal things but includes the overflowing power of the Holy Spirit.

Like filling up a hot cup of tea, God desires to fill us with His Holy Ghost fire, which brings His presence, light, power, and purification from everything that does not please Him. To experience an overflow of blessings, we must first be prepared to release anything that might obstruct the Spirit's influence. When we empty ourselves, allowing God to fill our hearts, we become capable of fulfilling His purposes in and through us. The boundless grace of God extends to those who fully dedicate their hearts to Him (2 Chronicles 16:9a). He intends to saturate us with His Spirit until our "cup overflows!"

Once you have emptied from your life the things that are not of God—such as sin, pride, or self-will—He can fill you up to overflow with His Spirit, His Word, and His provision. You will wholeheartedly be able to say: "I will never lack another day in my life! Come what may— calamity, famines, recessions, or any economic disaster—I shall not want! My supply will always be fresh and forever flowing. I have no worries about my present or future needs because I believe wholeheartedly that God's supply will never be exhausted!"

You may be experiencing tough times. You may be facing extreme debt or experiencing financial hardship. I have great news for you! If you turn your situation over to God, cry out, and repent if you need to for not being a good steward over your finances—watch God's goodness step in and overtake you. You will be overwhelmed with the goodness of the Almighty God.

Remember how Job was overwhelmed with troubles from left to right. His family, health, and finances were all attacked. But Job kept his faith in God. And after extreme testing of his faith, Job received double what he lost. God blessed Job with twice as much! Job was overwhelmed by the goodness of the Almighty God. If God did it for Job, He will do it for you!

One of the benefits of being a believer is God will show up for you! Even though you have been through the fire, you will come forth without smelling like smoke. So, get ready for your breakthrough! It will be so great that you will hardly believe it!

God's Benefits Package

Every time I sit down with a cup of hot tea, gratefulness wells up inside of me for all that God has done for me. Not only did He lead me out of debt, but He has provided for me so that I never need debt again! God is a deliverer and a sustainer. The world promises many benefits that can distract a believer and cause us to depend on man rather than God. We are bombarded daily with opportunities to "forget" or disregard all God can and will do for us.

Humankind tends to be more conscious of employment benefits, hourly pay, retirement packages, and insurance plans. And people seem to give more attention to the benefits of having a good credit score or good credit report than the unlimited ability of God to provide for His children. But believers need to know and remember the marvelous benefits we have in Christ and not forget them.

As beloved children of God, we have many precious benefits that exceed any "benefits package" from the world. In Psalm 103:2 (KJV), David encourages himself to: *"Bless the* LORD, *O my soul, and forget not all his benefits."* David stirs up his soul six times to remember and "forget not" all God's benefits. Here are a few essential benefits David reminds us we have in God: God forgives all our sins and casts them as far as the East and the West. God heals all our diseases. God redeems our life from the pit and destruction. God crowns us with lovingkindness and tender mercy. God satisfies our mouths with good things. The Lord executes righteousness and justice for all who are oppressed. The Lord is slow to anger, nor will He hold a grudge. The Lord holds back the punishment we deserve. He loves and has compassion for those who fear Him, and His mercy and lovingkindness are everlasting upon those who reverently fear Him.

What a good God! No earthly benefits can rival the extraordinary package of blessings that He offers. His divine "benefits package" surpasses anything human-made; it is filled with love, grace, mercy, guidance, and unending support. We must reflect on and remember the immeasurable goodness of the Lord. David's call to bless God becomes an invitation to acknowledge and appreciate the unparalleled richness of His blessings that transcend anything the world can provide. So, we ought to bless the Lord for all His benefits!

The Benefits of Tea

God is the source of everything good, including tea. And He gave me a desire for tea as a part of His benefits package. Psalm 103:5 (NKJV) says, He *"satisfies your mouth with good things so that your youth is renewed like the eagle's."* When I started drinking tea, I didn't know it had such unique medicinal and psychological health benefits. However, my favorite green tea is super healthy and contains antioxidants and other nutrients that protect the body and its cells against diseases.

Researchers also conclude that green tea slows down the natural aging process. And certain teas alleviate the symptoms of colds and flu, lower cholesterol, fight obesity, have antiviral and anti-inflammatory effects, and enhance memory. Tea may also help prevent stress-related diseases, including heart disease and stroke. Some studies have found that drinking black tea may lower the risk of cancer. Tea is even said to help relieve symptoms of depression. So, not only does tea taste good and help me relax, but it also has beneficial healing properties so that I am revitalized and renewed from the inside out.

Today, as I write, I am sipping my favorite peach-flavored green tea and reflecting on how good God has been to me. He lifted me out of a dreadful pit of debt, and I am so thankful! Regardless of my success, I will never forget that I once struggled in a horrible financial pit. But God showed up and turned everything around. I don't live in the past, and sometimes I wish I could leave the past behind, but there is a benefit in remembering what God has done for me. Even though I had strayed from the principles in His Word concerning money, He didn't leave or forsake me. Remembering how the Lord intervened on my behalf keeps me from ever going back. I will never return to the debt slave life again!

Throughout the Bible, God tells us to remember. In Exodus, God also tells the children of Israel to *"commemorate"* or remember the day He brought them out of Egypt from the slave life. God wanted them to remember what He had done for them (Exodus 13:3). They were not to forget where they came from or what the Lord had done for them. The Lord was taking them to a better place. But He didn't want them to get there and forget what He had done for them. Instead, God wanted them to look back and testify to His goodness, faithfulness, and kindness toward them. They were to pause and remember that He was the God of their salvation.

The Freedom to Sit and Learn

I find great joy in my decision to break free from debt. I am deeply grateful for the freedom it has brought me—the ability to sit peacefully with a cup of tea in God's presence without the burden of creditors, bills, or constant work to make ends meet. In freedom, I can pray and meditate with my mind free from anxiety about money. I can seek God's wisdom and walk in His purpose for my life. I have the peace of mind to hear God speak to me so that I can prosper and excel—His way!

Every time I sit down with a cup of hot tea, I am reminded of how God saved me from drowning in a sea of debt. I believe that another reason God gave me a love for tea is so I could take the time to remember what He did for me and bask in His presence. When drinking hot tea, you can't be hurried or busy doing things. To enjoy it, you must sit down and sip it slowly.

One morning, I sat down with my Bible and a hot cup of tea and came across the story of Martha and Mary in Luke 10:38-42. This story reminded me that Jesus is our ultimate source of freedom and rest. This story emphasizes the importance of being attentive and without distractions in His presence. The story unfolds with Jesus visiting Martha's home, and while Martha busily attends to household chores, her sister Mary sits at Jesus' feet attentively listening to His teachings. Martha spends all her time being distracted by her many tasks of serving her house guests. Perhaps she was preparing food for her guests or serving them water (or even tea). But Mary was giving her heart's affection and attention to the Lord.

Martha, consumed by her tasks, becomes frustrated and asks Jesus to make Mary help her. She said, *"Lord, don't you care that my sister has left me to do all the work by myself? Tell her to help me!"* (Luke 10:40) It is interesting that Martha wanted Jesus to force Mary to help her with busy work. But Jesus came to free us from a life of frustration and toil. Martha needed to take her apron off, sit at Jesus' feet, and learn to rest in Him. Unfortunately, she allowed busyness and the cares of the house to distract her. Martha was exhausted because she was doing all the work herself.

Jesus responded compassionately, pointing out that Martha was worried about many things, but only one thing was truly needed—to be present and receptive to Him. Mary had chosen the better path: Resting in Jesus and listening to His teachings, unburdened by needless distractions. Being at Jesus' feet represents a sense of quiet trust and reliance on Him. Martha had the choice to do the same but was busy checking off her to-do list. She didn't feel the freedom to stop her busyness long enough to receive a blessing from her house guest—Jesus.

Similarly, many of us get entangled in busyness, running after money and chasing material pursuits instead of prioritizing Jesus and His teachings. But Jesus says, *"Come to me... I will give you rest. Take my yoke... and learn from me, for I am gentle and humble in heart, and you will find rest for your souls"* (Matthew 11:28-29). Instead, we become anxious about the details of our lives when true peace comes when we seek Him with all our hearts. Trying to do things our way and using our limited wisdom only brings restlessness and disappointment.

We must intentionally take time to learn the correct way to live, like Mary, instead of constantly working and worrying, like Martha. Jesus welcomes anyone who is willing to sit, listen, and learn from Him. Jesus calls out to those who are hungry and thirsty for the right way to live to come to Him and be richly fed: *"Come, all you who are thirsty, come to the waters; and you who have no money, come, buy, and eat! Come, buy wine and milk without money and without cost. Why spend money on what is not bread, and your labor on what does not satisfy? Listen, listen to me, and eat what is good, and you will delight in the richest of fare"* (Isaiah 55:1-2).

It is in our best interest to heed this call. Those who are thirsty for what God offers will come to Him for everything we need without the burden of how to pay for it. The world wants to lend it to us; God wants to give it to us! Why exhaust ourselves by pursuing things that will never truly satisfy? When we prioritize seeking the kingdom of God and understanding righteous living, we are promised that everything else will fall into place.

God's abundant blessings and riches await those who align themselves with His voice, His Word, and His will. When we embrace and live according to biblical principles, we open the doors to supernatural provision and blessings that surpass our every need. By trusting in God's promises and abiding in His Word, we can confidently walk in debt freedom, freely live out our purpose, and generously help others. So, I encourage you to come out of debt, savor the sweet taste of financial freedom, and enjoy life's simple pleasures, such as a cup of hot tea!

Chapter 8

7 Spiritual Keys to Unlock Debt Freedom

T O ALIGN YOUR FINANCIAL LIFE WITH GOD'S will, you must embrace a lifestyle of submission to the Scriptures and the guidance of the Holy Spirit. You need unwavering faith in God's ways, acknowledging His perfection and the flawlessness of His Word (2 Samuel 22:31). I experienced a transformation in my finances by seeking wisdom from God, humbling myself, and adopting spiritual habits and discipline. To overcome a staggering $100,000 credit card debt, I cultivated daily spiritual habits, recognizing their importance for any committed Christian seeking financial freedom and a life that pleases God. These spiritual habits serve as keys that are readily available in the Bible and are capable of unlocking doors to answers and blessings in our lives.

The seven keys are prayer, praise, worship, fasting, Scripture, meditation, and confession. Utilizing these keys grants access to the necessary solutions that transform our mindset and behavior to align with God's Word and lead to prosperity and freedom.

I.   The Prayer Key

The first key is prayer, a powerful tool that can bring about significant changes. In my journey, I intensified my prayer life, especially in the mornings, as I faced my debt crisis. Instead of being consumed by worry, I sought God diligently through prayer and acknowledged His faithfulness in the past. Philippians 4:6-7 became my guiding principle, reminding me not to be anxious but to pray. I realized that anxiety arises when we try to control our lives without God's guidance.

In my prayers, I didn't simply ask for money to solve my problems; I sought God's wisdom and truth. Wholeheartedly, I cried out to Him, desiring to see and understand the reality of my financial situation. God answered my prayers, opening my eyes to two contrasting financial systems—the kingdom of God and the kingdom of darkness. I unknowingly entangled in the world's system by borrowing, contrary to God's principles. Through prayer, I gained insight into this truth.

By embracing prayer as a key, I unlocked the door to understanding God's will for my financial life. I realized that my situation required more than a quick fix; it needed a transformation of my perspective and actions. Through prayer, God revealed the path to debt freedom and financial alignment with His Word.

II.   The Praise Key

Praise is a powerful tool that grants us access to God's presence and opens doors that may have seemed closed and insurmountable. When we engage in praise, we draw God's attention, and our praise becomes a pathway into His court, where He hears our petitions and grants favor. We encounter the King through praise. Through praise, we bring God into our impossible circumstances. Praise causes doors of opportunity to swing open. During times of struggle and uncertainty, we should praise His great and holy name instead of succumbing to fear and self-pity. Psalm 34:1 (KJV) says, *"I will bless the Lord at all times: his praise shall continually be in my mouth."*

During my journey out of debt, I made praising God a daily practice, and I continue to do so. As I gained insight into His truth, my heart couldn't help but overflow with praise for His goodness and mercy. I understood that praise was one of the keys to my victory. I connected to God through my praise, and He *"delivered me from all my fears"* (Psalm 34:4). In moments of praise, I felt God's presence. Because I cried to Him with praise, He stepped into my situation and arranged supernatural solutions and resources. Psalm 34:19 (KJV) says, *"Many are the afflictions of the righteous, but the LORD delivers him out of them all."*

Praise brought me joy and peace despite my deep financial troubles because I knew God was working everything out for my good. I danced and praised in anticipation of my debt-free future, knowing God was faithful to fulfill His promises. My praise reached heaven, mobilizing God and His angels into action for my benefit.

I needed a breakthrough from God. So, when I say I praised God, I didn't merely sit in a chair with my hands raised shouting "Hallelujah." I was up on my feet dancing, stomping, and shouting around my house like I needed a move from God. In the Bible, we find inspiring examples of the transformative power of praise. King Jehoshaphat and his people praised God before a battle, and the Lord granted them victory over their enemies (2 Chronicles 20:22). When Paul and Silas were imprisoned and beaten unjustly, their prayers and songs of praise triggered an earthquake, setting them free (Acts 16:25-26). Similarly, the walls of Jericho crumbled when the Israelites praised God with shouts, allowing them to conquer the city (Joshua 5:13–6:27). King David praised God and danced with all his might in front of all his people because of the greatness and power of God (1 Chronicles 29:10-20; 2 Samuel 6:14).

Praise is not merely an expression of spirituality but a potent spiritual weapon. It scatters and destroys the enemy's schemes. My decision to praise God, even amid mounting bills and relentless creditors, played a significant role in my journey to becoming debt-free. I trusted that if God had shown up for others like King David, Paul, and Silas, He would also show up for me. God is consistent, unchanging, and impartial. Praise demonstrates our faith that the battle is already won, regardless of what our eyes see or what the natural world dictates. Praise moves the hand and power of God, making the impossible possible.

If you are facing overwhelming financial trouble, praise God relentlessly—like nothing else matters—until you witness the victory in your life. Things might look bad, but praise God anyhow! Praise will unlock the door to your financial freedom, just as it did for me.

III.   The Worship Key

Worship transcends mere praise; it emanates from a deep understanding and reverence for who God is. It goes beyond acknowledging His deeds to exalting His very nature. When we behold His greatness and power with awe, worship naturally flows. Revelation 4:11 beautifully proclaims: *"You are worthy, our Lord and God, to receive glory and honor and power, for you created all things, and by your will, they were created and have their being."* As beings created in His image, our design is to worship Him.

Worship is not confined to Sunday mornings in church; it should permeate our entire existence. While gathering for corporate worship is vital, worship is a lifestyle for believers. It entails aligning our thoughts and actions with God's desires and honoring Him in everything we do and say. The Apostle Paul described true worship in Romans 12:1-2 as presenting ourselves as living sacrifices, holy and pleasing to God. This requires renewing our minds to discard worldly wisdom and embrace God's truth in His Word.

God's Word is the ultimate truth in a world that embraces relativism. We must discern lies and deceptions that contradict His Word. Culture may advocate for credit and loans as a path to freedom, which leads to dissatisfaction and disappointment. Jesus alone can satisfy our deepest desires. Seeking Him, pursuing Him, and aligning with His truth will fulfill our expectations and needs.

True worship emerges from the heart of born-again believers. It goes beyond external actions to a spiritual connection with God. As Jesus stated in John 4:23, genuine worship occurs when our spirit unites with God's Spirit in truth. Studying God's Word grants us insight into His ways and exposes the truth. Recognizing that creditors provided my needs through credit and loans was an eye-opening revelation. Whoever I owe becomes my provider and object of worship.

The Scriptures remind us that "the borrower is a servant of the lender," emphasizing the importance of aligning our worship with God alone. We cannot serve both God and money. Instead, we are called to worship God with our resources, follow His stewardship principles, support our families, give tithes and offerings, help the needy, and share the gospel. When we worship God with our resources, we demonstrate our love for Him, acknowledging He is our ultimate source of provision and satisfaction. In this way, we elevate God above all else and live lives of true worship, finding fulfillment in glorifying Him.

IV. The Fasting Key

When I was in debt, I was under a lot of pressure. I needed a spiritual breakthrough and a financial breakthrough! I needed some spiritual food. So, it was time for me to put down my spoon and fork and focus on God. Even though I was seeking God in prayer, I knew that prayer and fasting together were keys to getting a response from the Lord. Fasting is giving up food for some time to focus your thoughts on God.

In the Bible, fasting occurred when the people of God endured personal challenges, a health crisis, financial turmoil, or other times of grief or distress. For example, King Jehoshaphat called for a fast in all of Israel when the Moabites and Ammonites came to wage war against them (2 Chronicles 20:3). Queen Esther and the Jews fasted when they faced genocide that was planned by Haman (Esther 4:3, 16). Even Jesus fasted for 40 days and 40 nights immediately after His baptism, before He started His public ministry, and before He was tested in the wilderness by Satan. Jesus demonstrated that fasting could help to strengthen us spiritually and help us endure temptation and trials.

I was facing an economic trial that I had never encountered before. So, I fasted more than ever before. My fast consisted of three full days without food or drink (not even water). I did no shopping other than necessary grocery shopping. I had no physical relations with my husband (with his prior approval), television, or casual phone conversations. I abstained from any self-centered activities. My purpose for fasting was to achieve a greater spiritual goal. I was saying "no" to my desires and pleasures and saying "yes" to God and His will.

Fasting is a way to declare mastery over our human nature (the flesh) so that we can live every moment led by the power of the Holy Spirit. Through fasting, I removed the distraction of food because I needed spiritual nourishment from the Lord. I told God I needed Him and trusted Him to deliver me from my trouble.

While fasting and seeking the Lord, I received God's wisdom, revelation, and directions. As I read the Scriptures, I could understand with more profound clarity. Fasting is a spiritual tool and a weapon against conforming to the world's ways. I realized I was deeply entangled in the world's system and needed to repent. In the book of Joel, God commands the rebellious Israelites to return to Him through fasting: *"'Even now,' declares the LORD, 'return to me with all your heart, with fasting and weeping and mourning.' Rend your heart and not your garments. Return to the LORD your God, for he is gracious and compassionate, slow to anger and abounding in love, and he relents from sending calamity. Who knows? He may turn and relent and leave behind a blessing"* (Joel 2:12-19a).

Fasting is essential to a financial breakthrough. As you humble yourself before God, you realize you need His help. God promises that if we return to Him and remove unrighteousness far from us, He will return to us, pardon us, and restore us (see 2 Chronicles 30:9; Isaiah 55:7; Job 22:23).

When I fasted, I could hear the Holy Spirit more clearly tell me things to do that led me out of my situation. Because my mind was clearer, I could better determine God's will for my life and had the wisdom to make critical decisions. Fasting allows you to draw closer to God in the Spirit and opens the door to answers you may not receive any other way.

V.   The Scripture Key

For believers, the Bible is our most crucial resource, providing guidance for living according to God's ways. Within its pages lie instructions, principles, and methods that lead us to succeed in every aspect of life. As God's image-bearers, we were created to have dominion, victory, and triumph! However, we may lose our way when we try to navigate life without God and His Word as our guide. Thankfully, the Scriptures are a lamp for our feet and a light for our path, illuminating the best instructions for living a successful life that pleases God (Psalm 119:105).

In Joshua 1:8 (NKJV), we find a powerful promise: *"This Book of the Law shall not depart from your mouth, but you shall meditate in it day and night, that you may observe to do according to all that is written in it. For then you will make your way prosperous, and then you will have good success."* By immersing ourselves in God's Word and aligning our lives with its teachings, we open ourselves to His plan for prosperity in every area—including our souls, health, and finances.

The Scriptures affirm that God "gives us the power to get wealth" (Deuteronomy 8:18) to fulfill three primary purposes:

- Meeting the needs of our households
- Supporting the Gospel and Kingdom work
- Exercising dominion on earth

To avoid financial pitfalls and debt accumulation, we must change our beliefs about money by becoming rooted in prayer and deeply studying God's Word. The Word has the supernatural power to renew our minds, transform our lives, and liberate us from conformity to the world's ways. It is not just words on a page. God Himself is the living Word (John 1:1), and Scripture is alive, active, and powerful (Hebrews 4:12). Through its divine inspiration, Scripture teaches the truth, corrects our paths, and keeps us from danger and stumbling away from God.

As devoted Christians, we should love the Scriptures. Meditating on God's law and commands should be our daily delight (Psalm 119). When faced with the world's contrary messages, we respond with the written Word in our hearts. Through Scripture memorization, we arm ourselves against temptation, declaring the truth in the face of deceit. Therefore, let us hold fast to the Word, for it is our sword and shield, guiding us to a life that pleases God and leading us to success and prosperity in every aspect of our journey.

VI. The Meditation Key

When I faced the overwhelming burden of being over $100,000 in debt, my mind was consumed with worry day and night. Peace seemed elusive, but I found solace and tranquility even amid the storm as I turned to Scripture. Through prayer, reading God's Word, and meditating on His promises, I discovered a peace that surpassed understanding and the knowledge that I could trust God to provide for my every need. Despite the turmoil of bills and creditors, I was assured that God would see me through.

Meditation on God's Word was pivotal in my journey to debt freedom. As I pondered His promises and attributes, I understood His overwhelming love for me. Trust in the Lord blossomed within me, bolstered by the Holy Spirit's help in comprehending and living out the Scriptures. My thoughts aligned with God's, and my actions reflected the truths I found in His Word. When the Bible instructed us to "owe no man anything but love," I embraced it as a path to financial success, and I committed to getting out of debt by fully relying on the Lord.

Psalm 119 emphasizes the significance of meditation in the life of those blessed by the Lord. Meditating on God's precepts, decrees, and commands becomes a source of delight and guidance. Biblical meditation is distinct from New Age practices; it is not about mystical rituals or chants but rather about contemplation, reflection, and dwelling on biblical truths. Through meditation, we detach ourselves from the world's influence and attach to God's thoughts and Word, recognizing when our thoughts deviate from His.

Just as God prepared the new generation of His people to enter the Promised Land with the wisdom of His law, we can also experience success and prosperity by immersing ourselves in the Scriptures. God exhorted Joshua to meditate on His Word day and night, and God promised that obedience would lead to blessings and prosperity. Psalm 1:1-3 illustrates that true success and wealth come from delighting in God's law and meditating on it consistently, leading to a fruitful and prosperous life.

VII. The Confession Key

Confession of God's Word is vital to attaining financial freedom. While the term "confession" may often evoke thoughts of admitting sins, it goes beyond that. It is also a profession of faith. To confess is to agree with God by declaring our heartfelt belief in His truth. In Greek, the word "confess" is *homologeo*, meaning to say the same thing as God. By speaking God's Word, we align ourselves with His promises and purposes.

The very Word of God brought forth the creation of the universe. In Hebrews 11:3, we learn that God framed the worlds with His Word, calling things into existence from nothingness. The power of His spoken Word brought light into being. Just as God's words have creative power, our words also hold significant influence.

By confessing God's Word daily over our financial well-being, we build our faith and protect our spirits from doubt and fear. Confession empowers us to trust that God will provide for us. We break free from the world's self-help systems of credit, debt, and loans, discerning the deceptive influences of the current economic climate that oppose God's purposes.

Debt freedom may seem impossible—like moving a mountain. But what did Jesus say to do when you are facing a mountain? He didn't say run from it, hide from it, climb it, nor did He tell you to wait on God. Instead, He said, *"Speak to the mountain"* (see Mark 11:23-24).

You can move the mountain of debt from your life! If you want to be debt-free, stop using debt! Then start saying, *"I owe no man anything but love, according to Romans 13:8."* Say it until you are out of debt entirely. Your confession will cause things in your life to obey your words. If you truly believe the words you say, you will automatically stop behaviors that cause you to owe money. You will begin to despise credit card debt. You will hate paying interest. Your spirit will convict you against doing things not aligned with your beliefs. Finally, things will begin to line up so that you can get out of debt.

Your words have power! So, speak the Word! Even if you don't feel anything happening, watch what you say because "death and life are in the power of the tongue" (Proverbs 18:21). Speak what you desire to see, not the problems you currently face. Don't speak negative thoughts such as, "I will never get out of this debt," or "It's impossible to live in this world without debt." Instead say, *"I am out of debt, and all my needs are met!"*

Say what God says about you. As a believer, you can confess that *"wealth and riches are in my house"* because that's what the Word says in Psalm 112:3. Say it even though you haven't seen it or have it yet. Your words should reflect what you want, not your present circumstances. When you believe and speak in line with God's Word, you release a force that changes the circumstances in your life.

Confession is an expression of faith and agreement with God's truth. It increases our confidence and dispels fear. As we study the Word, we discover all God has for us, and we can boldly confess His promises. When facing daunting challenges, rather than declaring impossibility, we look to God and proclaim, *"If God is for me, who can be against me?"* (Romans 8:31).

Daily confession of God's Word empowers us to face any circumstance with courage, knowing that we are more than conquerors in Christ. Economic uncertainties will not shake us, for we trust the One who holds all things in His hands. With unwavering faith, we declare, *"God will take care of me and supply all my needs according to His riches!"* Confession becomes the expression of our faith in action, setting the stage for the manifestation of God's promises in our lives.

Chapter 9

7 Practical Principles
for Mastering Your Money

Principle #1: God Owns Everything

THE FOUNDATION OF MASTERING YOUR MONEY lies in recognizing that God is the ultimate owner of everything. From the beginning, God created the heavens, the earth, and everything within them. All things, including us, were made by Him and for Him (Genesis 1:1; John 1:3). We are not owners, but stewards entrusted with managing His possessions. God delegated authority to humankind to govern and control His creation, but He retained sovereign ownership.

Psalm 24:1 reminds us, *"The earth is the Lord's, and every-thing in it, the world, and all who live in it."* While we may have legal titles to property or possessions, we must grasp that these are temporary and will not accompany us beyond this life. The bottom line is, *"We brought nothing into this world, and we will carry nothing out"* (1 Timothy 6:7, paraphrased). Have you ever seen a U-Haul truck hooked to a hearse taking belongings to the cemetery? None of your possessions have any value after you die. All land, houses, cars, furniture, money, toys, electronics, and gadgets will be left behind. You can't take it with you!

Understanding God's ownership is crucial for our financial journey. It reminds us that money is not our possession, but a resource entrusted to us by God. He tests us to see if we will be responsible with a little before He trusts us with a lot. Our handling of money reveals what we prioritize and love the most. We demonstrate genuine faith by being responsible stewards of God's resources.

As custodians of God's resources, we are responsible for managing His wealth with utmost care. Every financial decision we make holds spiritual significance. Our call is to bring honor to the Lord in all aspects of life, including our finances, as stated in 1 Corinthians 10:31. Jesus serves as our model, glorifying the Father in every aspect of His life, inspiring us to dedicate all areas of our existence to God's glory.

Recognizing that our money belongs to God transforms our approach to spending, saving, and investing. Each financial choice becomes an opportunity to honor and magnify Him. While God desires us to enjoy the blessings of wealth, we must also approach our financial practices with prayer, discipline, and responsibility.

Principle #2: Stewardship

A core principle in mastering your money is understanding the concept of stewardship. As believers, we are not owners, but stewards of all God entrusted to us. Stewardship involves wise management and responsible care of everything that belongs to God, including financial resources, possessions, time, talents, and influence. Like a manager overseeing a company, we have been given the privilege and authority to govern and control God's assets for His purposes and glory.

Embracing stewardship requires a mental shift from an owner's perspective to recognizing ourselves as caretakers of God's blessings. We enjoy the benefits of His provisions, but nothing truly belongs to us. Our role is to seek God's wisdom and will in every financial decision, aligning our choices with His Word and principles.

Money serves as a test of true discipleship, revealing what we love and trust the most. A good steward prioritizes God above all else and uses money in a way that brings glory to Him. A faithful steward is not consumed by selfish interests; instead, they manage resources with a focus on glorifying and magnifying God. Living debt-free and embracing generosity are vital aspects of responsible stewardship. Our financial choices reflect our devotion to Christ and the extent to which we honor Him with our resources.

God's ownership of everything changes how we perceive and handle money. The Parable of the Talents illustrates the importance of increasing and multiplying the resources entrusted to us. A good steward diligently seeks to grow what God has given, recognizing that faithful management leads to greater responsibilities and blessings. Misusing or wasting God's resources goes against the principles of stewardship. The Parable of the Prodigal Son reminds us of the consequences of squandering wealth without careful planning and responsible behavior.

We must resist conforming to the world's ways and instead allow the truth of the Gospel to shape our financial habits and attitudes. Embracing stewardship aligns our financial decisions with God's will, ensuring that we use money as He intends and for His glory. As faithful stewards, we seek to manage God's resources wisely, knowing that our choices have present and eternal consequences. God desires us to grow and increase what He has given, using it to bless others and fulfill His purposes. Our stewardship reflects our faith and trust in God, and it is a key aspect of living out the Christian life with integrity and devotion to our Master.

One day, God will call us to give an account of how we managed what He has entrusted to us. Ultimately, we should aspire to hear, *"Well done, my good and faithful servant."*

Principle #3: Be Content with What You Have

The Apostle Paul is an inspiring example of someone who found contentment in all circumstances, whether in abundance or need. Despite facing harsh treatment and various challenges, Paul's joy and sufficiency came from his deep relationship with God. He knew he could rely on Christ's strength to sustain him even in tough times.

Contentment does not mean that you cannot desire to change your circumstances in life, but it means you should be satisfied with what you have in the present. It involves finding peace and satisfaction in our present circumstances while pursuing growth and advancement with gratitude and trust in God's provision. Hebrews 13:5 (ESV) says, *"Be content with what you have, for he has said, 'I will never leave you nor forsake you.'"* Being content with what you have does not mean that you must keep the same car forever or that you should never desire a new house. However, if you are not positioned financially to buy the latest or biggest, be content with what you have today. If you need something, pray and believe God will provide.

Scripture reminds us that God will never leave or forsake us, and His promises should be the foundation of our contentment. While wealth and possessions can be uncertain and fleeting, our trust in the Lord provides security and comfort. When we lean on God's promises, we can resist the temptation to fret about future needs and avoid the desperation that leads to unwise financial decisions, such as borrowing to fulfill immediate desires.

Paul emphasizes that contentment does not mean neglecting to take action or plan for the future. Instead, it means recognizing that our essential needs are met through God's grace and provision. Trusting in Him allows us to seek His will for our lives and confidently pray for the things we need, knowing He will always take care of us.

Contentment also involves avoiding the trap of coveting what others have. Comparing ourselves to others and striving to keep up with their perceived success leads to dissatisfaction and discontentment. Instead, we must focus on God's unique plan for our lives and be grateful for the blessings He has bestowed upon us.

In today's world of social media and constant exposure to others' lives, it's easy to feel envious or dissatisfied with our own circumstances. However, it's crucial to remember that what we see on the surface may not reflect the full reality of others' lives. Coveting what belongs to someone else leads to a restless pursuit of material possessions and can drive us into unnecessary debt and financial ruin.

The key to contentment is prioritizing God and His Word, ensuring that our hearts are not captivated by the pursuit of material possessions or worldly success. Seeking fulfillment in people or artificial things will always leave us unsatisfied and unfulfilled. Instead, we must seek God's will and trust that He will provide for our needs in His perfect timing.

Principle #4: Keep Out of Debt

Living with debt has unfortunately become the norm in our society, encompassing personal, business, and government debt. Credit cards, mortgages, loans, and student loans are common ways people accumulate debt to fulfill their desires and needs. The ease of borrowing money has made it tempting to buy now and pay later, leading to a lifestyle filled with stress, anxiety, and financial burdens. The allure of instant gratification often leads people to spend beyond their means, accumulating debts that can become overwhelming and detrimental to their financial well-being.

Debt allows us to acquire things before we can truly afford them, and this instant gratification often leads to a cycle of increased spending and lifestyle inflation. As our income rises, so does our desire for more—perpetuating a never-ending pursuit of material possessions and worldly success. The credit card industry lures us with attractive offers that encourage us to overspend and live beyond our means. Convenience checks and cash advance offers make it too easy to indulge in impulsive purchases and accumulate more debt. However, these seemingly sweet deals come at a significant cost in the long run, primarily because of the added interest.

The path to financial freedom starts with seeking guidance from God's Word. A clear and practical principle emerges from Romans 13:8: *"Keep out of debt and owe no one anything."* This command applies to all forms of debt, whether personal, business, or mortgage related. God desires us to love one another, not be enslaved by financial obligations. When we accumulate debt, we become servants to our creditors, bound by the need to work extra hours and take on additional jobs or hustles to make ends meet. Many believers are so busy working to make money to fund their lifestyle or simply to make ends meet that they don't have time for a relationship with God—to pray, seek, or serve Him. You will either serve God or serve money.

Solomon wisely reminds us in Proverbs 22:7 that the borrower becomes a servant or slave to the lender.

Borrowing money may seem like a means to make more money and achieve success, but it often leads to financial instability and vulnerability. Trusting in God's blessings rather than borrowing is the key to financial prosperity. When we obey God's command to keep out of debt, we position ourselves for His blessings and provision.

Living a debt-free lifestyle may require a shift in mindset and priorities. Instead of focusing on material possessions and worldly success, we should prioritize God's will and trust in His provision. Letting go of the reliance on borrowed money brings mental and physical relief, allowing us to regain control of our time, energy, and finances. Trusting in God's provision and living by faith brings security and peace of mind.

A debt-free life is characterized by wise financial choices, discipline, and a belief that if we don't have the money to buy something, we don't need it. Embracing contentment with what we have and living within our means will free us from debt and open opportunities for greater financial freedom.

Embracing a debt-free lifestyle is not about depriving ourselves of the good things in life but about aligning our choices with God's principles. It is a journey that requires faith, discipline, and a willingness to let go of the world's standard of success. By exercising self-control and spending only what you have, you can break free from the shackles of debt, pave the way to a secure financial future, and foster a sense of peace and confidence in your financial decisions.

I released a ton of mental and physical pressure when I decided to stop using credit cards and loans to finance my expenses. I gained control over my financial situation and future. I found security in spending no more money than what I have and trusting God to meet my needs. My financial motto is: "If I don't have the money to buy it, I don't need it! And if I want it, I will believe God for it!"

Principle #5: Create a Financial Plan

To be good stewards of our finances, we need a well-thought-out spending plan that aligns with God's will and glorifies Him. Such planning ensures financial stability, guards against impulsive decisions, and empowers us to make choices that honor God.

The foundation of any financial plan should be prayer. Before making any commitments or financial decisions, seeking God's guidance through prayer is crucial. A prayerless approach can lead to mistakes and compromise our values. Billy Graham said, "A prayerless Christian is a powerless Christian." Turning to God in prayer allows us to align our decisions with His will and invites Him to be an integral part of our financial journey.

Before you build a house, start a business, pursue higher education, buy a car, or whatever you plan to do, you should first sit down and plan and ensure you have enough to finish what you started. In Luke 14:28, Jesus says that a man should *"count the cost."* Unfortunately, many individuals undertake ventures without fully comprehending the costs or adequately assessing the necessary resources, leading to unfinished or unattainable outcomes. You must evaluate the challenges and potential obstacles you might face to be adequately prepared to see the endeavor through to completion. Jesus says in Luke 14:28 (NKJV), *"For which of you, intending to build a tower, does not sit down first and count the cost, whether he has enough to finish it—lest, after he has laid the foundation, and is not able to finish, all who see it begin to mock him, saying, 'This man began to build and was not able to finish?'"* Starting a project should not be taken lightly, especially if you are a believer. People are watching what you do. They may see your unfinished work and mock and ridicule you.

A good financial steward does not start something he or she can't finish due to lack of money and necessary resources because this does not bring glory to God. The phrase "count the cost" emphasizes the significance of making informed, thoughtful, and wise decisions. Having a financial plan is vital to managing our money effectively and helps us avoid unfinished projects and financial mismanagement.

To create a financial plan, we must be aware of our financial situation, which requires knowing the extent of our debts and assets. By thoroughly assessing our financial standing, we can begin formulating a plan to accomplish our financial goals and eliminate debt. Writing down our income, expenses, and debts is essential to controlling our finances and preventing overspending.

The Bible says, *"Write the vision and make it plain on tablets, that he may run who reads it"* (Habakkuk 2:2, NKJV). I prefer a hand-written financial plan to be kept in a notebook or folder. That's what works for me. But you can use a phone app or financial software. Figure out what is best for you and stick to it.

You need three essential documents in your financial plan: a debt worksheet, a statement of net worth, and a spending plan.

Debt Worksheet

Because I was in so much debt, the first step I had to take before looking at my net worth was to add up my debt obligations. Discovering how much I owed was a fearful and painful process. But the only way to change my situation was to know where I stood financially. So, first, I needed to know where my money was going.

I got a copy of my credit reports from the three major credit reporting agencies: Equifax, TransUnion, and Experian. Each credit report was different and revealed debts that were not on the other. Then, I wrote a list of all my creditors, the total debt I owed, and the due dates. If you are in a lot of debt, which is very emotional for you, consider seeking a financial coach to help walk you through this vital step. You can find a debt worksheet form to download and print out on my website at www.michelleelliottministries.org.

Statement of Net Worth

Before I created a spending plan, I compiled a statement of net worth, which provided a comprehensive overview of my financial standing—including my assets and liabilities. This summary offered a clear snapshot of my financial health and laid the groundwork for planning to achieve my God-given financial goals and dreams.

In the net worth statement, I meticulously listed the value of all my assets and then subtracted my liabilities or debts owed. The resulting figure revealed my total net worth. Unfortunately, the outcome was disheartening as I had no assets or positive net worth, only burdensome liabilities. Confronting this reality helped me understand the consequences of my previous reckless financial behavior and motivated me to change directions, moving toward debt freedom. You can also find a statement of net worth form to download and print on my website at www.michelleelliottministries.org.

Spending Plan

While some may associate budgeting with constraints, it is essential to view it as a spending plan that aligns with our income and values. A spending plan empowers us to intentionally direct our money where it should go, preventing wastefulness and aligning our finances with God's principles. Taking control of our spending through a well-thought-out plan helps us break free from debt and progress toward our financial goals. Creating a spending plan is essential in ensuring that your expenses remain within the limits of your income, which is the fundamental principle for achieving financial success and freedom—always spend less than you earn.

A spending plan has a category where you fill in your income and monthly expenses. It has categories that address every area of cash flow—including housing expenses, utility bills, transportation costs, insurance, entertainment, travel, tithing, giving, and more. The key is to be prayerful about each category and allow God to lead you. And when you commit to the LORD whatever you do, He will establish your plan, and your plans will succeed (Proverbs 16:3). You can find a spending plan document to download and print out on my website at www.michelleelliottministries.org.

Spending less than you earn is a vital principle for financial success. By adhering to this principle, we can free up money to pay off debts and save for the future. Paying with cash or debit instead of credit can help curb impulsive spending, making us more aware of our purchasing decisions. Understanding that our money belongs to God motivates us to spend wisely and prioritize needs over wants.

As believers, we are called to live differently from the world, even when managing money. Our spending plan should reflect biblical principles—including tithing, helping those in need, avoiding debt, and saving money. By aligning our money management with God's Word, we honor Him and experience the financial freedom He desires.

Principle #6: Save for the Future

Saving for the future is a crucial principle emphasized in the Bible. We demonstrate responsible stewardship by saving instead of spending all our resources. Saving money prepares us for future opportunities and enables us to be better prepared for unexpected emergencies. Shockingly, studies reveal that more than half of Americans—including Christians—lack sufficient savings to cover minor unforeseen expenses, which leads many to rely on debt to meet their needs. Proverbs 21:20 says, *"The wise store up choice food and olive oil, but fools gulp theirs down."* A person who is foolish with money doesn't set any aside but unwisely eats it up or consumes it all.

The Bible teaches us to learn from the ants that diligently prepare during times of abundance for the leaner times that may follow: *"Go to the ant, you sluggard; consider its ways and be wise! It has no commander, no overseer or ruler, yet it stores its provisions in summer and gathers its food at harvest"* (Proverbs 6:6-8). Ants have no leader, chief, or ruler, but they work hard and store their food during the summer in preparation for winter. They know and anticipate that winter is coming when they cannot work outside. So, they take advantage of the summer months, preparing for the colder, harsher months.

Ants have the foresight to work together to prepare for hard times, but many humans stand back unprepared for an economic downturn, a recession, or other personal financial situations. The Bible calls such people sluggards or lazy people who love leisure and end up with nothing. A sluggard is unwilling to work hard and doesn't take responsibility for his own life.

In the story of Joseph in Genesis 41, we see a powerful example of being prepared for the unexpected. Upon receiving God's warning that there would be seven years of plenty followed by seven years of famine, Joseph wisely stored grain and resources during the plentiful years, ensuring that there would be plenty of provision for the future. By saving during the years of plenty, Joseph helped maintain stability and order during the famine. When the famine hit, Joseph was prepared. He could provide for the surrounding countries, including his own family in Canaan. Joseph's good stewardship of resources caused him to be ready to meet not only his own needs but the needs of others.

Preparing for the unknown may seem challenging, but establishing a savings plan is a practical step toward financial security. While we cannot predict the exact nature of future economic conditions—like a recession, inflation, or a pandemic—we can build a safety net that will protect us and allow us to help others in need.

Prioritizing saving is an essential element in attaining financial success. It gives us confidence to navigate life's uncertainties and shields us from falling into financial turmoil. Regardless of the economic situation, relying on debt to meet our needs adds tremendous mental, emotional, and financial strain on us and our families. However, a well-established savings plan can diminish our dependence on debt during critical situations like job loss, medical emergencies, or unexpected expenses. Maintaining emergency and long-term savings creates a protective cushion to handle unforeseen circumstances, thereby liberating us from debt and granting us peace of mind.

Principle #7: Giving Is Living

God is the greatest giver of all time! The generosity of our heavenly Father knows no bounds, as He selflessly and mercifully provides for us in countless ways. From the gift of life and breath to the truth of the Gospel, God showers us with His blessings and graces, even bestowing His Spirit to reside within us. He equips us with everything we need for a life of godliness.

Giving isn't just a good idea—it's God's idea! In James 1:17, we are reminded that every good and perfect gift comes from above, flowing down from the Father. The ultimate display of God's love is seen in the sacrifice of His only Son, Jesus, on our behalf. This act of love sets a model for His people to emulate by giving sacrificially and generously to those in need.

In 1 John 3:16-18, the Bible emphasizes that genuine love is expressed in words and actions and truth. Our compassion should extend to our brothers and sisters, especially those in need. When we withhold help from those in distress, it casts doubt on the presence of God's love within us.

Giving is not merely a suggestion; it is an expectation for followers of Christ. God delights in cheerful givers, and our acts of generosity mirror His character. As Jesus stated in Acts 20:35, *"It is more blessed to give than to receive."* When we give through tithes, offerings, or helping the less fortunate, we sow into God's kingdom, and He multiplies our resources in ways we cannot fathom.

The act of giving, whether in times of abundance or scarcity, is an act of faith that demonstrates our trust in God as our ultimate provider. By sowing seeds of faith, even during challenging times, we open ourselves to God's miraculous intervention and provision.

If You Have a Need, Sow a Seed

Sowing and reaping are fundamental principles of God's kingdom. Just as a farmer expects a harvest after planting seeds, believers can anticipate God's blessings as they sow into His work. It might not happen immediately, but the Bible promises that a harvest will come as surely as day and night exist. A habit of generous sowing results in constant blessings and supernatural increase as God's multiplication power is activated.

When I found myself in a boatload of debt, God taught me another form of giving—His system of sowing and reaping. This may surprise you, but before I got out of debt, I would receive large amounts of money into my hands, and God would tell me to give the money away! It surprised me, too! I thought, "Why would I give money away when I need money to pay my debts!" But I was facing insurmountable debt and needed a miracle. So, I began to see in the Scriptures where God required a seed before He met a need because planting is an act of faith.

Sowing during a time of famine, during a recession or economic downturn, or in your own financial crisis is a powerful demonstration of faith. It gives God a mighty opportunity to prove Himself and to show Himself strong on your behalf. In Genesis 26, the Bible says that Isaac sowed during a famine. In the same year, Isaac reaped 100 times more than what he planted! Some people may not believe you can trust God for a 100-fold return on your giving, but Jesus discussed it in Matthew 13:23 and Mark 4:20. The Bible says that Isaac gained more and more until he became very wealthy. Isaac owned many flocks, herds, and servants (Genesis 26:12-15). Isaac trusted God during a famine, not just during times of plenty, and while others were hungry and losing possessions, he was multiplying and increasing.

Sowing seeds is a demonstration of your faith. A seed is a resource we can plant by faith and cause God to release His multiplication power. While I was still in debt, money would come into my hands, but it was never enough to pay off my debts. So, I decided, "If it's not enough for my need, it must be a seed." It takes faith to let go of money when your needs are so big. But I was beginning to trust in God and not money! I was learning that the kingdom of God operates through *sowing and reaping,* not lending and borrowing. So, I had to tap into giving so I would never have to borrow again.

While I was still in debt, most of the money that came through my hands became seed money. I asked God what He would have me do with it. And I waited for the Lord to tell me where to sow, and that's how I knew it was good ground. One time, I was given $1,000 cash. God immediately told me who to give it to. I didn't give it a second thought and laid it at the man of God's feet. Even though I was up to my neck in debt, I obeyed God's direction about when and where to sow. When I planted my seed, I didn't see what was happening naturally, but I believed God was working out my debt situation in the supernatural realm.

Every time I sowed, I was demonstrating that money didn't have a hold on me, but God was my source. When I planted a seed in obedience and faith, God moved on my behalf and opened the door to my debt freedom. I realized that the way to overcome lack and dependence on debt was through sowing seed!

For years, I had tried to get out of debt. My family couldn't help me. My friends couldn't help me. My college degree couldn't help me. I knew it wasn't a job or more income that would get me out. The interest was accruing faster than a paycheck could cover. I needed a miracle! I stopped using credit and loans and started sowing seeds. My debt cancellation came because of my seed. I sowed my way out of debt! I showed God that I trusted Him more than the world's resources. When I planted my seed in faith, the anointing of God broke loose, and God's burden-removing, yoke-destroying power went to work on my behalf. After I was obedient in sowing seed, I received ideas and opened doors that led to my debt deliverance!

Sometimes, God asks us to do things that don't make sense, but they make faith. When God tells us to give, if we obey His instructions, the results are always positive and work for our good. For instance, in 1 Kings 17, I learned faith, obedience, and generosity lessons from the widow woman. This widow was broke. All she had left to her name was a handful of flour and a small amount of olive oil. She was preparing to cook the last meal for herself and her son when she encountered the prophet Elijah. She was sure they would die of starvation. But Elijah told her to first "sow" some of the meal to him. And he promised her, *"The jar of flour will not be used up, and the jug of oil will not run dry until the day the Lord sends rain on the land"* (v. 14). So, by faith, the widow did what she was told, and a miracle happened! As promised, the widow had enough daily food for Elijah, herself, and her family!

This widow didn't have enough for her needs, so she turned what she had into seed! Rather than eating her seed, she trusted God with it.

A Higher Way of Living

I discovered a mystery, a secret of the kingdom of God. *A seed can change any condition!* Seedtime and harvest are God's plan to take us from needing debt or loans to a higher way to live. The Bible tells us in Genesis 8:22, *"As long as the earth endures, seedtime and harvest, cold and heat, summer and winter, day and night will never cease."* So, when you sow a seed, as long as day and night still exist, you can count on a harvest coming. Yet, people are often discouraged from sowing because their seed does not produce an immediate crop.

Cultivating a habit of constantly sowing seeds brings constant blessings. Sowing and reaping is God's divine plan for increase and multiplication. Jesus even speaks of the hundredfold return in the Parable of the Sower: *"And these are they which are sown on good ground; such as hear the word, and receive it, and bring forth fruit, some thirtyfold, some sixty, and some an hundred"* (Mark 4:20, KJV). In this parable, Jesus is speaking of sowing the Word. But when you sow a seed, that's how it works. You can expect a multiplied harvest! So, if you have a need, plant a seed!

Some years ago, when I started gardening, I began understanding how seedtime and harvest work. I took one tiny tomato seed, sowed it into some fertile soil, and watched it grow. I didn't know how the seed would grow, and I had no idea when I would see any tomatoes. I just had faith that tomatoes would grow. I put the seed in the ground and waited for it to sprout. I was amazed that one tiny seed brought many tomatoes on one vine. It was a miracle!

A farmer plants a seed expecting to receive a harvest of much more than he sowed. If he sows a watermelon seed, he expects watermelons to grow. The farmer doesn't know how or when the harvest will come, but he is patiently looking and expecting! It's out of his hands. It's a mystery. All by itself, the soil produces what the farmer sowed without help. You can read more on Jesus' teaching on the seed in Mark 4:26-29.

Believers must understand that the kingdom of God is a seed kingdom. It operates by sowing and reaping and giving and receiving. In contrast, the kingdom of this world is a debt kingdom. It operates on buying and selling and lending and borrowing. In this world system, when you invest, you may incur significant losses. The world's economy and markets fluctuate up and down depending on many outside influences, such as supply and demand, inflation rate, unemployment rate, imports and exports, and other variables. However, God's kingdom operates according to the power of a seed.

When you are faithful in your giving—whether tithes, offerings, helping those in need, or cheerfully planting seeds in good soil, you will prosper according to His Word! When you give and invest in the kingdom of God, it will be given back to you—multiplied and in good measure, pressed down, shaken together, and running over (Luke 6:38). Jesus has promised that if you give, more will be given to you.

God Gives Seed to the Sower

God taught me firsthand that He *"gives seed to the sower"* (see 2 Corinthians 9:10). One day, I went to a restaurant with my husband and children. I left my purse in the car for some reason—I usually never do that. But as soon as we got to the counter to sit down, I noticed a $20 bill on the floor. Nobody was around it, so I picked it up. I immediately heard the voice of God say, "Give it to the server." I knew the money I found was not to replace our tip. IT WAS A SEED! I also heard God say, "I give seed to the sower." That's when I discovered why I had left my purse in the car. I didn't need it. God gave the seed.

That day, I learned that God provides everything we need—the seed, the soil, the rain, and the harvest. God gives seed to the one who will spend it on what He says to do with it. So often, people have a seed but spend it on something they want. You will never prosper from sowing if you consume or "eat up" your seed. Sowing isn't always easy. It can hurt a little at first, but you must decide in your heart to sow, and it gets easier.

God is the ultimate provider! He provides the seed and the soil for the farmer to plant, sends the rain, and multiplies the seed to produce an abundant harvest. The more you sow, the more the Lord will cause you to overflow in abundance (2 Corinthians 9:8-10). Opportunities, ideas, and directions will come your way; and doors will open to you, leading to your increase. When you obey God in your finances, blessings and resources will come to you and overtake you!

Giving isn't just a good idea! Giving is living! Abundant living in the kingdom of God is intricately linked to the principles of giving and receiving. While it might seem unconventional or contrary to worldly norms, generous giving plays a pivotal role in God's grand design for our financial well-being. He invites us to give with the purpose of blessing us, enabling us to be a blessing to others, and actively participating in the advancement of His kingdom on earth.

When we sow into God's kingdom, we can expect to reap abundant blessings and provisions from the very kingdom we contribute to. When we sow into the kingdom, we reap from the kingdom: *"Remember this: Whoever sows sparingly will also reap sparingly, and whoever sows generously will also reap generously. Each of you should give what you have decided in your heart to give, not reluctantly or under compulsion, for God loves a cheerful giver. And God is able to bless you abundantly, so that in all things at all times, having all that you need, you will abound in every good work"* (2 Corinthians 9:6-8).

The kingdom of God is a seed kingdom. God doesn't ask you to give money, time, or resources to take from you or burden you. When you give, He desires to bless you in such abundance that you have everything you need—and so much more. When you give bountifully, you will reap bountifully! God will enrich you, not just in money but in all things. Second Corinthians 9:11 says, *"You will be enriched in every way so that you can be generous on every occasion."* God will richly bless you so that you can give, at a moment's notice, whenever there is a need—which brings thanksgiving to God! People will thank God because of your giving to them.

Unlimited Prosperity

Giving activates God's unlimited supply. Sowing seed in good ground, wherever God tells you to sow, will unlock the door to unlimited prosperity and financial freedom! If you tap into seedtime and harvest, sowing and reaping, you will never have to depend on the world's financial system of lending, borrowing, credit, and loans ever again! You will never have to run after money. It will come after you! First, however, you must decide that God is your source—not financial institutions!

Sowing is the key to prosperity! As you purpose in your heart to give into the kingdom, nobody will be able to stop your flow of blessings, and it will be unexplainable! You will leave debt and lack behind when you understand and operate in God's seed kingdom. Neither your paycheck, savings account, 401K, stock portfolio, pension, or social security checks are any match for sowing and reaping. When you become a bona fide sower, you will live on another level and in a greater dimension of God's blessings. You will activate heaven's supply, and you will never be broke again another day in your life!

Chapter 10

Recovering Everything You Lost

D ECIDING TO LIVE DEBT-FREE CAN BE SCARY AND intimidating. If you are in a lot of debt, like I was, you may wonder, "How will I ever recover from this?!" The journey out of debt is not easy, but it's worth it! Right now, you may feel embarrassment, shame, and economic hardship. But God knows how to give you beauty for ashes, turn your mourning into joy, and turn your despair into praise. God knows how to take the ugly parts of your life story and turn them into something beautiful. He did it for me, and He'll do it for you!

Throughout the Bible, when the people of God turned away from Him, He withheld His blessing. It happened to Adam and Eve. They were exceedingly blessed but disobeyed God and lost everything. They lost their relationship with God, were evicted from their garden home, lost their wealth, and so much more. The world and humankind are still dealing with the chaos and disorder resulting from their decision to disobey.

But all is not lost. God has provided hope through His Son, Jesus Christ. God sent Jesus to rescue us, recover all losses, and restore everything we lost while we were backslidden and ignorant. Colossians 1:13 (NLT) reminds us, *"For he has rescued us from the kingdom of darkness and transferred us to the Kingdom of his dear Son."* He came not only to save those *who* were lost but also to recover *what* was lost. Most Christians fail to understand the magnitude of what Jesus redeemed back for us. He didn't just die for the forgiveness of our sins or to give us a ticket to heaven. There is more to salvation than that. On the cross, Jesus defeated Satan and took back a seven-fold blessing!

Jesus took back everything the devil stole! We have been forgiven, redeemed, and restored! We were delivered from all sin and brought into freedom. God's plan of redemption is the total restoration of all that was lost in the fall of humanity. What Adam lost in the Garden, Jesus undid on the cross! We are no longer bound to live under the curse of this world's system of sin, debt, and bondage. Jesus is our Jubilee! He paid our ransom. We have been released—like a kidnapped person, like a slave freed from bondage!

It was for freedom that Christ set us free. We no longer must live with debt. Our debts were not only forgiven but wiped out! And when we accept Jesus as our personal Lord and Savior, we receive an inheritance—the *"unfathomable riches of Christ"* (Ephesians 3:8, NASB). The devil tries to blind us and keep us from receiving our birthright, but the Lord will pay us back big time!

Recoup Years of Losses

I was in so much debt that I didn't know how I would recover. However, it wasn't long after I got out of debt that a prophet of God told me and my husband that we would "get back everything we lost." I immediately believed what the prophet said. The Bible says, *"Have faith in the LORD your*

God, and you will be upheld; have faith in his prophets, and you will be successful" (2 Chronicles 20:20). I also found verses in the Bible that confirmed that God would not only restore us, but we would recover better than before! For example, I found a verse in Jeremiah 33:26 where God says, *"I will restore their fortunes and have compassion on them."* I was encouraged that even though I drifted away from His Word, God is full of mercy and promises to restore those who turn back to Him.

The sin in our lives can devastate our health and wealth. Still, God promises in Joel 2:25-26 if we turn back to Him, we will recoup years of losses: *"I will repay you for the years the locusts have eaten—the great locust and the young locust, the other locusts and the locust swarm—my great army that I sent among you. You will have plenty to eat until you are full, and you will praise the name of the LORD your God, who has worked wonders for you; never again will my people be shamed. Then you will know that I am in Israel, that I am the LORD your God, and that there is no other; never again will my people be shamed."*

When God restores, He does not merely restore you to the way you were before you experienced sin, brokenness, or failures, but God's restoration leaves you better than ever. He restores you to a place of recovery and wholeness. God's promise of restoration is always in abundance. Jesus says, *"The thief comes only to steal and kill and destroy; I have come that they may have life and have it more abundantly"* (John 10:10).

Satan's servants, ministers, and minions use temptation and deception to rob believers of the truth concerning money. Don't be deceived. The Bible calls him *"the devil and Satan, the deceiver of the whole world"* (Revelation 12:9-10), *"the ruler of this world"* (John 12:31), and *"the god of this age"* (2 Corinthians 4:4). He comes in undetectable ways. And if you don't keep your spiritual eyes and ears open, you can be fooled. He is like a bandit or pickpocket who steals and takes what he wants and is long gone before the person is even aware that he was ever there.

Satan comes disguised as an angel of light (2 Corinthians 11:14). He is our adversary, and his mission is to keep God's people ignorant of the spiritual truths in the Bible. For instance, I am speaking to you today through this book telling you that the Word says, *"Keep out of debt and owe no man anything."* Then Satan immediately says, "You can't live in this world without debt." Satan will disguise his voice to make you think God is talking to you. He wants us to believe a lie that is disguised as the truth. It is the same trick he used on Eve in the Garden.

Satan has fooled many believers like he fooled Adam and Eve. This world system of debt seems right. But it robs you of the blessed life. Satan can't stand the fact that you are blessed. He wants to rob you blind. Satan wants to rob you of your faith in God and keep you from your inheritance. He will stop at nothing to steal your joy, your peace, your freedom, your time, and all your money.

The devil stole from me for years while I was ignorantly in debt. But the Bible says, *"Anyone who steals must certainly make restitution"* (Exodus 22:3). Restitution is payment for injury or loss. In a criminal case, a judge may order a criminal to pay restitution to the victim when the crime causes the victim to endure financial loss. For example, a victim may be compensated for out-of-pocket expenses, lost wages, or medical expenses. The purpose of restitution is to make victims whole financially—as they were before the crime. Restitution holds offenders accountable for losses suffered by the victims of their crimes. In the same way, the Bible says that if a thief is caught, *"he must pay sevenfold, though it costs him all the wealth of his house"* (Proverbs 6:31). So, when a thief has been found stealing to increase his sustenance or wealth, he must pay! He must return what he has stolen seven times.

It was a considerable amount when I thought about what my husband and I lost to get out of debt and get right with God. When I added up the value of the car we sold, the investment properties we gave up, and the income we lost, our total losses were well over a million dollars! The devil deceived me and stole from me in my ignorance, and I endured significant losses, but he must compensate me for his theft. So, I live every day expecting to receive back money, land, and property—valued at millions of dollars!

Satan had a plan to destroy Job's life. Job lost everything— his children, health, and wealth—but maintained faith in God. The Bible says God restored Job's fortune and gave him twice as much as he had before. The Lord blessed the latter part of Job's life more than before (Job 42:12). Job got double for his trouble!

Likewise, the Israelites were held in slave bondage by the Egyptians for many years. But when the children of God were delivered from Egyptian slavery, they would not leave Egypt broke or "empty!" God judged the Egyptians, stripped them of their wealth, and the children of God came out of their oppression with great wealth and possessions (Psalm 105:37). They left Egypt with restitution and financial recovery for all their troubles!

Don't Give Up

One of the greatest enemies of faith is a lack of patience. Satan will pressure you to make you think God's Word isn't working. The truth is that *the Word never fails*. But many times, when there is a delay in what we are hoping for, we tend to get weak-hearted and give up on waiting for it to happen. The pressures of the world will make you think God won't come through. So, you worry 24 hours a day about money and how you will make it. If you allow stress about money to consume your mind long enough, you will return to that world system that seems so easy and reliable.

In Mark 4:19, Jesus says, *"But the worries of this life, the deceitfulness of wealth and the desires for other things come in and choke the word, making it unfruitful."* Be careful not to turn away from the truth and allow money pressures and the deceitfulness of riches, the pleasures of life, or materialism to choke the Word and cause you to fall back into a debt cycle. Don't give up.

Often, we want to rush through our waiting season. If we do this, we may not learn essential lessons or fully develop our trust in God. When you decide to live debt-free, you must also determine that you will not succumb to pressure to go back in. Life's pressures will entice you to throw away your confidence in God. But don't do it! Don't be moved by anything except the Word of God.

After I got out of debt, I was free, but I didn't experience all the promises of God right away. I had to continue to walk by faith and not by sight. I continued to take one step at a time. I diligently sought God's kingdom and prioritized His Word in my life. While I waited on God to fulfill His promises, I continued to get educated in what the Bible says about money and debt. I purchased every word-based financial freedom book, DVD, and sermon series that I could get my hands on. I learned personal money management skills, such as how to create a budget, ways to track spending, and how to develop a savings plan. I also increased my understanding of financial investment tools such as insurance and real estate. I was preparing to stay out of debt and for the coming blessing.

Don't give up on God—even if nothing seems to be working. Instead, encourage yourself in the Lord. Strengthen yourself in the Word. David is an excellent example of someone who encouraged himself in the Lord even though all seemed lost. In 1 Samuel 30:1-19, David was in distress because the enemy, the Amalekites, invaded his camp and ripped him off. While David and his army were away at battle, the enemy came in, raided the city of Judah, took everything, and then burned down the town of Ziklag. The wives and everyone else in the camp had been abducted. David was in a terrible situation. David and his army cried out until they had no more tears to cry.

Have you ever been so distressed that you cried until you couldn't cry anymore? Many people are in this kind of distress because of debt! However, the Bible says that David found strength in the Lord! David called on the name of the Lord for answers! He didn't just sit there weeping and mourning. He got up and got ready to fight for what belonged to him.

The best way to fight is with the Word of God. You must encourage yourself with God's promises that declare you already have the victory. If you are in a bad situation and things don't look like they are working out, open your Bible to Psalm 34: *"This poor man called, and the LORD heard him; He saved him out of all his troubles. The angel of the LORD encamps around those who fear Him, and He delivers them"* (vv. 6-7). And when your needs seem overwhelming, turn to Psalm 23 and find your strength where it says, *"The LORD is my shepherd; I shall not want"* (v. 1). It is with the Word of God that you fight and win! In the end, David went into the enemy's camp and took back everything that had been taken! The Bible says David recovered ALL!

Even if you are facing some tough financial challenges, say this: *"I will recover all!"* Keep believing and speaking it. It may take some time, but you will recover if you don't faint or give up. Even when things look impossible, don't quit. God works best in impossible situations! Stand firm and resist the urge to go back into debt. Your faith will get tested. Satan won't let you out of his system without a fight. But even when things get tight and even if you lose some things, don't get pulled back into that failing system. You will experience the goodness of the Lord if you faint not.

Receive a Hundred Times More!

In Mark 10:29, Jesus assures us that anything we give up to live in righteousness is a gain, not a loss! We must be willing to let anything go to follow Him. God calls us to give up anything we love more than Him. You might have to let the house go if God didn't lead you to buy it anyway. Your debts and obligations keep you from serving God. You may need to let a lot of stuff go anyway.

Jesus promises that anyone who suffers loss to follow Him will receive back far more than they will ever lose! If you lose your house—don't worry! If you must give up a car because you can't afford it—don't worry! Whatever you give up for the sake of the Gospel, Jesus says you will receive back 100 times as much: *"Truly I tell you,"* Jesus replied, *"no one who has left home or brothers or sisters or mother or father or children or fields for me and the gospel will fail to receive a hundred times as much in this present age: homes, brothers, sisters, mothers, children and fields—along with persecutions—and in the age to come eternal life"* (Mark 10:29-30). Jesus says you will get back one hundred times TODAY—in this present age. That means you don't have to wait for heaven to enjoy life.

No matter what you must give up, don't worry—He can bless you exceedingly more than you could ever think, hope, or imagine! You have only seen a "snippet" of what God has for you!

Everybody won't agree with your decision to live debt-free, and that's okay. You may be criticized or ridiculed for your decision. But the Bible says, *"Blessed are those who are persecuted because of righteousness, for theirs is the kingdom of heaven"* (Matthew 5:10). On your way to the top, you may lose some family members and friends. But don't worry. You will gain the most incredible family—the family of God! And if you are willing to leave behind worldly wealth to follow Christ, you will be significantly compensated for your sacrifices. You will recover and gain *true riches*.

Ultimate Freedom and Rest

Achieving financial freedom requires discipline, planning, and making wise financial choices. Like savoring a cup of hot tea, it signifies the time to appreciate life's small moments without the burden of financial stress. By breaking free from debt obligations, you can attain a life of rest, tranquility, security, and overall well-being.

In today's fast-paced and unpredictable world, with the rising cost of almost everything, anxiety and stress about provisions are widespread. Believing that God will supply all your needs is an antidote to these emotional burdens. People of faith must rely on the Word of God to guide their financial decisions rather than conforming to the ways of this world. It is unwavering faith in God that brings about ultimate freedom and rest.

As believers, we must trust our needs to God the Father. He is our divine source of support and care. When you believe that your needs will be met, it reduces anxiety and alleviates materialistic obsessions so you can focus on what truly matters: fostering meaningful relationships, practicing love and compassion, and doing good in the world.

In Christ, you will find all you need and everything you ever wanted—freedom, peace, rest, wealth, family, land, houses, AND eternal life!